Barnet at War

Barnet at War

PERCY REBOUL

AND

JOHN HEATHFIELD

ALAN SUTTON PUBLISHING LIMITED

First published in the United Kingdom in 1995
Alan Sutton Publishing Limited
Phoenix Mill · Far Thrupp · Stroud · Gloucestershire

British Library Cataloguing in Publication Data

A catalogue record for this book is available from the British Library.

ISBN 0–7509–1038–0

Cover Picture: Nos. 142 to 146 Crescent Road, East Barnet, were hit by a bomb in
1941. This is believed to be Mrs Bozier, who lived at No. 146. It is typical of the
English to give high priority to pets. Note the shoes standing on top of the
suitcase.

Typeset in 11/12 Erhardt.
Typesetting and origination by
Alan Sutton Publishing Limited.
Printed in Great Britain by
Ebenezer Baylis, Worcester.

Contents

Acknowledgements and Sources

Local sources have included the minutes and committee reports of Barnet, East Barnet, Friern Barnet, Finchley and Hendon councils, all of which are held at the Barnet Borough archives. They also have a good set of air raid report forms and civil defence log books. We have read the *Finchley Press* (1936–46) and the *Barnet Press* (1939–45), numerous ephemeral magazines and the log books of a number of local schools.

Several official publications have proved essential for background reading. They are:

B. Collier, *The Defence of the United Kingdom* (HMSO, 1957)

T. O'Brien, *Civil Defence* (HMSO, 1955)

R. Titmuss, *Problems of Social Policy* (HMSO, 1950)

Anon, *The Front Line 1940/41* (HMSO, 1941)

The archives of Mass Observation (the first organization to attempt to obtain some kind of objective view of people's behaviour) are available at Sussex University. Some of the material has been published and has been used in our preparation.

This has been supplemented by the written and oral memories of a number of people. We wish to thank Laurie Adams, W. Allibone, Doug Austin, George Curtis, Olive Dyke, Ted and Brian Heathfield, Jack Prime, Don Robbins, Stan Springate, Maud Swain, Sister Lourdes, Donovan Smalley, Dennis Reboul, Cyril Fletcher, Doris Hammersley, R.M. Franklin and especially Joanna Corden, Pamela Taylor and Jill Barber of the borough's archives department.

We also thank STC, now Northern Telecom, and the head teachers of Cromer Road, Underhill, Woodhouse and All Saints schools. We are grateful to Finchley Memorial Hospital for permission to publish extracts from *Your Hospital in War*.

Revd Patrick Henderson helped clarify our thinking. Liz Holiday and Bill Gelder helped by making many useful comments.

In particular we would like to state that although the book is published in cooperation with Barnet Council, all opinions are those of the authors and nothing in the book should be taken as necessarily representing the policy of the council.

The authors have taken care to contact all possible sources for permission to use copyright material. If any such material has inadvertently been used without permission, the authors would be grateful to be told, care of the publishers.

'I suppose in about thirty years' time people will insist on describing this as the good old days.'
A cartoon from Punch

Introduction

Just over fifty years ago, during the Second World War, the area known today as the London Borough of Barnet was under attack from the air with high-explosive and incendiary bombs. The attacks were not as catastrophic as had been originally feared, but they were bad enough and served as a daily reminder that the area, like the rest of Britain, was fighting for its very survival. This is a story of those times.

The great issues of the Second World War have been discussed endlessly by professional historians, generals and politicians, but much remains to be recorded about how ordinary people, those we regard as our neighbours, felt and acted during those traumatic years or how they were organized for war.

An important part of our story concerns the time prior to the outbreak of war in September 1939. We all know, with hindsight, the eventual outcome of the conflict but we need to remind ourselves that it was a close run thing. When war broke out, Britain was in many ways ill-prepared, badly led politically and full of fear about what was going to happen.

At the time, films and photographs of recent wars in Spain and Ethiopia, along with memories of the hideous carnage of the First World War, seemed to confirm the official line that 'the bomber will always get through'. This gave rise to a widely held belief that the towns and villages of Britain would be reduced, virtually overnight, to heaps of rubble. Such fears were compounded by the notion that the ultimate horror, poison gas, would be used against any of those lucky enough to survive the initial bombing. The coming war, in effect, would be the abominations of the First World War visited upon the unprotected citizens of this island.

In addition, the Barnet area faced special problems. Many Jews and political refugees, who had fled their homelands because of Nazi persecution, settled in areas such as Hendon, Golders Green and Hampstead Garden Suburb. Their different languages and cultures caused some antipathy among the local population and their lives were made even more difficult by traditional British attitudes to 'foreigners' and the fear of spies among their numbers.

It is most astonishing that, in spite of this nightmare scenario, the people of our locale, in common with the rest of Britain, put such fears behind them and buckled down to a total war effort.

Morale, the will to resist, was strong at all times – even during the height of the air raids. There was an unshakeable conviction, not without justification as it transpired, that on our own ground Britain's navy and airforce could match that of the enemy. With 'right' on our side and backed by the might of the British empire, it was argued, the final outcome would never be in doubt. Such illusions, if illusions they were, were encouraged by the world's finest propaganda machine, called the Ministry of Information, and, in a short space of time, a charismatic war leader, Winston Churchill.

We feel that some explanation is needed about the choice of locations for our story. The London Borough of Barnet, of course, was not in existence in the war years. As we show, civil defence and much else besides was based largely upon the then district and county councils working closely within ground rules laid down by the national government. What was true of Finchley, therefore, would be mostly true of Hendon, Mill Hill, Edgware and other parts of today's borough. To minimize repetition we have tended to concentrate on the northern part of the area: Finchley, Friern Barnet, East Barnet and Chipping Barnet. In so doing, we recognize that this will not please everyone, even though we refer to particularly important events in other areas. What is certain is that the residents of all areas of today's borough shared the suffering and triumphs of those years. It is to all of them that this book is dedicated.

Percy Reboul
John Heathfield
London, 1995

Barnet at War

ONE

The Path to War

It was the First World War, with its air raids on London and elsewhere, that brought home to the British people the fact that wars were no longer just fought abroad by members of the armed services. Henceforth, civilians would be in the front line of battle. Britain was no longer an island.

In 1933 Adolf Hitler became Chancellor of Germany. Smarting under what he and others considered the humiliating peace terms of the First World War, he committed Germany to a massive rearmament programme which included the development of new generations of fast bomber aircraft planned to give his Third Reich overwhelming air superiority. Britain and France and the other countries in the League of Nations could not find an effective way of curbing the growth of German power and of preserving peace in Europe. A policy of appeasement was adopted that was ruthlessly exploited by Hitler and his war machine.

But no government, however misguided, could afford entirely to ignore all the evidence of German intentions. The British people did not want war and viewed unfavourably any measures that might be taken to rearm the nation or prepare for war – particularly if it involved spending any money. The views of unpopular politicians such as Winston Churchill, who argued for action, went unheeded. It seemed advisable, however, to commit plans to paper and a sub-committee of the Imperial Defence Committee was formed in 1935 to consider the situation.

The committee recognized two major problems: the need to record key areas and installations that would be at risk (docks, railways, aerodromes, power stations and the like); and the need to devise a system that would give protection against air raids. The latter was called Air Raid Precautions – ARP for short. Later, in 1941, it was renamed Civil Defence.

Some of the committee's conclusions and findings seem, with hindsight, both strange and wide of the mark. For example, it concluded that in the first two months of war there would be 1,800,000 casualties of whom over half a million would be dead. This would require 20 million square feet of timber per month for coffins. This was felt to be too expensive so mass graves and the burning of bodies in lime were authorized. Equally bizarre were its comments about how the various social classes would perform under fire. 'The working classes', it opined 'are bound to crack, run, panic and even go mad, lacking as they do the courage and self-discipline of their masters or those regimented in the Forces of the

Crown.' As it transpired, the working classes performed heroically under fire and one of the few positive outcomes of the war was that different classes tended to band together to fight the common foe, thereby breaking for a time the noxious attitudes to class.

In 1935 an ARP department was formed at the Home Office to take over the work of the Imperial Defence sub-committee. News of this move was made public and consultations took place with local authorities to discuss and agree the machinery of civil defence. Suggestions and appeals appertaining to this, however, fell mainly on deaf ears because no provision was made for financing by the government. With such an example, local councils were hardly likely to want to increase rates to pay for what they saw as a national responsibility. They were, after all, an elected body and, as such, needed to uphold the views of their supporters and safeguard their finances. Private firms too were reluctant to pay for this 'national concern'.

Most local authorities saw their mandate as one which discussed the problems and committed them to paper. This was better than nothing and, in fact, some remarkably apt schemes were devised. One authority (not in Barnet), for example, identified the need for first-aid posts, casualty clearing stations, base hospitals, stores, gas decontamination and repair squads, street wardens, despatch riders and reserve firemen. The most likely explanation of this degree of sophistication would seem to be that this authority listened to those with first-hand experience of the First World War.

As international tension built, the government could no longer avoid the issues and it passed the first ARP Act in 1937. This provided money for those local councils who had expressed an interest in civil defence – the sums available based on the weighted population of each area. The most severe problem was seen as poison gas and work which had started in 1936 continued on the manufacture of a gas mask for every member of the population including young children and babies.

Other action included the development of an air-raid warning system – the well-known siren to indicate 'alert' and 'all-clear'; a system of 'blacking out' all streets and buildings; and plans for the evacuation to the countryside of non-essential personnel from towns and cities. First aid and rescue services were combined and a Civil Defence Reserve formed. Most important for the future were changes planned for the fire services, which, at that time, were under the control of individual local authorities. Greater coordination, expansion and planning of the service was certainly required but even these changes were to prove inadequate when the air raids finally came. In spite of the utmost gallantry of firemen during the Blitz (as it became known) there were shortcomings in the organization which were not rectified until the service was nationalized in 1941.

Perhaps the most vital decision taken at the time was that civil defence should be organized on a decentralized basis. This meant that borough councils and county councils could build their civil defence requirements and programmes around existing local organizations and trained personnel, who had unrivalled knowledge of their area and the loyalty to match it. Britain was divided into regions, each one of which was to be headed eventually by a regional officer and one clerk. Their main job, in those early years, was to inform and encourage local authorities to take an active part in civil defence matters.

Another topic considered was the need for an air-raid shelter which could survive almost anything except a direct hit. The famous Anderson shelter, made from corrugated metal, was intended to be erected 'in the back garden'. The fact that millions of Britons did not have a back garden seems not to have occurred to the planners. A later improvement was the Morrison shelter, erected in the house, and public surface shelters made from brick and concrete. Other vital plans included schemes for a National Registration Identity Card and food rationing for the whole population.

MUNICH AND AFTER

In February 1938 Hitler annexed Austria and the mood of the British people began to change in the light of this fresh menace. The authorities, previously reluctant to show warlike intentions, could now make more open preparations, and interest in civil defence began to grow. In June 1938, for example, the Public Health Committee of Finchley Council issued a clearance order for the purchase and demolition of Nos 1,123–45 High Road, Whetstone. They offered the buildings to the ARP Committee for practice purposes (see below).

On Saturday 20 May 1939, as part of the training for war, a Blenheim light bomber flew over Whetstone High Road in a simulated bomb run. Whetstone Place, the terrace of derelict houses shown here, was set alight in order to practise fire fighting and rescue techniques. Unfortunately it was some time before a satisfactory blaze could be established.

How to erect an Anderson shelter. It was essentially a simple job.

The so-called 'Morrison' shelter was made of strong steel and was used by many families as a dining table. It provided a secure indoor refuge provided that it was placed on a strong floor.

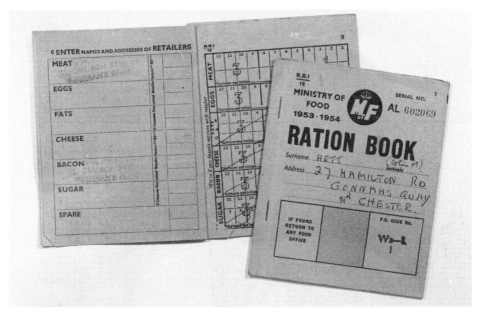

This ration book, although for use after the war, differs little in design and content from those issued originally in 1939 (see p. 54).

Paperwork and bureaucracy flourished in the war years. These are just a few of the documents needed.

> ## FRIERN BARNET URBAN DISTRICT COUNCIL.
>
> # AIR RAID PRECAUTIONS.
> ## A PUBLIC MEETING
> will be held in the
> ### Church Hall, Friern Barnet Lane, N.11,
> on
> ### Tuesday Next, May 3rd, 1938, at 8 p.m.
> The Chair will be taken by
> ### COUNCILLOR J. E. PICKERING, J.P.
> (Chairman of the Friern Barnet Urban District Council),
> supported by
> ### COUNCILLOR A. C. HENRY
> (Chairman of the Friern Barnet Air Raid Precautions Committee)
> and other Members of the Council.
> *Speakers :*
> ### FLIGHT-LIEUTENANT EARDLEY WILLMOTT
> (Home Office Inspector of the London Area)
> and
> ### LIEUTENANT-COMMANDER A. THURLOW, R.N. (Retd.)
> (Air Raid Precautions Officer, Friern Barnet).
> Arrangements will be made to enrol Volunteers for
> the various Sections at the conclusion of the Meeting.

Recruiting campaigns for the ARP were already underway, albeit slowly, well before the outbreak of war.

The minutes of the ARP Committee of Barnet Urban District Council for April 1938 reported that 218 persons were now under training as air-raid wardens in four centres in Barnet and that double that number was estimated to be required. A further thirty-two volunteers would shortly be established in Totteridge and Woodside Park. The St John Ambulance Corps had sixty-three members fully trained in first aid. Instructions into ARP matters were arranged for members of the council's fire brigade and recruitment for the auxiliary fire service was in hand via posters and advertisements in local newspapers. The council's 'outside staff' were also being trained in techniques of poison gas decontamination.

A Hertfordshire County Council exercise on 5/6 May 1938 revealed many shortcomings, and training programmes were arranged to remedy them. A nationwide 'black-out' practice, which involved putting out all street lights, caused so many traffic accidents, and there was so much burglary and associated crime that, when war eventually broke out, a modified form called 'dim out' was used.

It was in 1938, too, that another vital piece of the defence jigsaw was put in place – the Women's Voluntary Service. The Home Secretary of the time, Sir Samuel Hoare, approached Lady Reading about recruiting women to help with ARP work. At the end of that year nearly 300,000 women were recruited: they were soon to become a vital part of the war effort.

BRINK OF WAR

In September 1938 yet another political crisis occurred, which brought Europe to the very brink of war. Following further German aggression, the British naval, land and air forces were mobilized and gas masks issued to the whole nation. Prime Minister Neville Chamberlain flew to Munich to meet Hitler. Together with the French Prime Minister Daladier and the Italian dictator Mussolini, he signed a peace accord with Hitler – the infamous 'piece of paper . . . that would guarantee peace in our time'. The relief in Britain was immense but the people of Britain were not deluded: they knew it was a temporary respite and threw themselves with increasing vigour and enthusiasm into training and preparation for war.

On 20 April 1939 the Home Office wrote to all local councils instructing them to accelerate their preparations for war and that civil defence was to take precedence over all other council business. Not least of those preparations was the finalization of plans to evacuate children and other vulnerable groups. Our local councils accordingly set up special committees to look after areas such as food rationing, fuel, allotments, fire brigades and billeting. Other council departments such as surveyors and engineers were expanded. The responsibility for most of these tasks was placed on the shoulders of the town clerks.

Civil defence control centres were organized. In Hendon, Friern Barnet and East Barnet, these were located in the basement of the town hall; Finchley's centre was in the basement of Avenue House and Chipping Barnet's in the council offices in Wood Street. These centres were the hub of civil defence plans and drew together the various strands. They housed maps of the area and used tally boards to show the strength and disposition of their forces to meet each incident. They had both GPO and direct telephone lines to series of wardens' posts (see p. 13) with messengers standing by at all times should the lines be damaged.

Many of these facilities involved making alterations to existing features and incurring financial costs, even before any war had started. At Avenue House, for example, the necessary alterations cost £48 plus £68 for extra telephone lines. An emergency exit, comprising a 30 inch diameter concrete pipe, was installed in the basement and led out into the grounds. The centre at Friern

The basement of Friern Barnet Town Hall included a purpose-built Civil Defence control centre, seen here under construction in 1938.

Barnet town hall, planned during the building of the new town hall in 1938, was not finished until 1943 – the final bills for the whole building were not paid until 1945.

Various back-up and reporting centres were also built, the one for Barnet at the old Dissenter's Chapel in Totteridge Lane, and the one for Middlesex as a whole in the basement of Woodhouse School, Finchley. A bomb disposal squad was also housed at the school in the early part of the war.

New staff were recruited. Friern Barnet, for example, appointed Mr P.H. Treadgold as Technical Assistant (Civil Defence) at a salary of £275 a year. Teachers at this time earned between £250 and £300 a year. The pace of training accelerated. Training centres were established with various courses in civil defence. For instance, the whole staff at Cromer Road School in Barnet, together with many other teachers, attended a first-aid course at East Barnet School. The training centre for Friern Barnet was at 'Strathay' in Friern Barnet Lane and Finchley used St Mary's School, Hendon Lane, and Avenue House as their training centres.

Equipment for civil defence was in much demand throughout the country and items were delivered piecemeal as and when they became available. Finchley Council, for example, reported that the waiting list for equipment varied from six weeks to nine months. In April 1939 the Home Office delivered 195,000 sandbags to protect civil defence establishments, and by November 1939 (two months after

The evacuation of children and other vulnerable groups away from likely danger areas had been planned well before the outbreak of war. This publicity picture was taken in September 1939. Finchley and Barnet were reckoned to be safe areas and as such received evacuees from other parts of London. It was not until 1944 that the V1 and V2 campaign changed that view.

the start of war) 82 per cent of clothing and 88 per cent of heavy equipment had been received.

The first real traumas of war were to be experienced in the first days of September 1939, with the evacuation of children and other vulnerable groups from the cities. As we have seen, the plans for this had been long prepared and involved the use of trains, buses, cars, coaches and even ships. Much of today's London Borough of Barnet was far more rural then and was not considered a particularly vulnerable area. Many wealthier families, however, made their own private arrangements and, later, a few children were included in the Children's Overseas Reception Board Scheme (CORB), which arranged for five to sixteen-year-old children to be evacuated to the Dominions and USA. This programme came to a tragic end when the *City of Benares*, carrying children to Canada, was sunk by a U-boat and seventy-three children were killed. Although, with

In an attempt to reduce horrendous facial and other injuries caused by flying glass, the windows of schools and other public buildings, homes and all kinds of public transport vehicles were covered with adhesive fabric or sticky paper crosses.

hindsight, we can see the massive over-reaction to the threat from the air, the authorities of the time were as much concerned to keep the roads clear of refugees and panicking civilians.

On 3 September 1939, following Hitler's invasion of Poland, Britain and France declared war on Germany. The ultimate test of local preparations for war was about to begin.

TWO

In the Front Line:
The Attack from the Air

Following the evacuation of British troops from France (the so called 'Miracle' of Dunkirk), Britain stood alone against Hitler's Germany. On 7 September 1940 and for the four succeeding weeks, London was submitted to an ordeal by bombing such as the world had not seen up to then. This period of daylight bombing and the following months of night bombing came to be called the Blitz.

Hundreds of German bombers dropped about 13,600 tons of bombs on London. In 1940, 13,596 Londoners were killed; 6,487 were killed in 1941. A further 18,378 casualties were admitted to hospitals. London was now in the front line of the conflict. The detailed figures for the whole war in our various districts are set out in the Appendix.

The gun site at Sweets Nursery between Oakleigh Road North and Friern Barnet Lane at Whetstone. The eight 4.5 inch heavy anti-aircraft guns fired a shell weighing about 50 lb to a height of 8 miles. The primary purpose of the barrage was to force enemy planes to fly too high for accurate bombing.

THE WARDEN SERVICE

At the heart of the Civil Defence organization was the control room, linked by telephone, and if necessary by messenger, to the wardens' posts and emergency services. Roughly speaking, there was one wardens' post for every thousand people.

In Friern Barnet, these posts were built by the Raglan Building Company at a cost of £59 each. They measured 8 ft by 6 ft by 8 ft high, with 13 inch brick walls and a 12 inch reinforced concrete roof. They were equipped with 3 chairs, 1 table, a 15 watt electric light bulb, a 40 watt radio receiver and a 600 watt electric fire. Most also soon acquired a dart board. Not all wardens' posts were purpose-built, however; sometimes they occupied rooms in people's houses or in garages. If a house was used, the government paid a rent of 5s (25p) a week. Hendon had 113 wardens' posts, which were all built by the same firm, Messrs Garsubil.

The ARP warden, who in pre-war years had been regarded as something of a figure of fun, was vital to the whole system of civil defence. He or she had two distinct roles to play; to be the eyes and ears of the control centre and the 'good neighbour' in the event of trouble.

A senior full-time warden was generally in charge of each post. Supporting him, on a 24-hour-a-day, 365-days-a-year rota, were other full- and part-time wardens, serving in the early days on a voluntary, but later on a compulsory, basis.

The view from Hadley looking south towards London at the height of the Blitz during the winter of 1940/41.

Warden's post number one, district A, in East Barnet Civil Defence Area, was on Hadley Green opposite Dury Road. Like most others it was purpose-built of 13 inch brick walls with a 6 inch reinforced concrete roof. Only a few remain today. Warden Garnett is on duty.

Inside a typical warden's post. The warden on the left is filling in details supplied by the other warden, who has just returned from the incident. Radio warnings of a possible invasion or similar emergency would have been received on the wireless set on the upper shelf.

This official photograph of a group of Hendon wardens is remarkable because there are no women present. This was not typical of the Warden Service, nor of the Civil Defence effort as a whole. Back row, left to right: H.G. Jennings, M. Silverman, S.N. Levy, R.J. Bonner, R. Kerr, W.R. Walters, M.P. Britton, A.J. Thwaites. Second row: P.F. Hayward, L.G. Fluke, A.V. Sully, S.B. Swan, F.J. Pay, E.A. White, A.E. Jones, A.F. Reeve. Front row: L. Levy, W.R.C. Lait, H.H. Glover, G.L. Collins, W.C. Ramsay (Chief Warden), R.H. Templeman, J.A. Bridger, S.A. Jenkins, G.T. Beattie.

Duty shifts were normally for twelve hours. Up to twenty-four wardens were needed to ensure cover.

There was a wide mix of social classes among the civil defence workers. The wardens of District A of East Barnet included Leslie Holt, the District Warden, a retired bank manager, an accountant, a hydraulic engineer, the verger of Hadley Church, a butterscotch maker, a bacteriologist, a golf club groundsman, a company director, a builder, a stockbroker, a painter and decorator, a university professor, a solicitor and his chauffeur, a stockman, a hairdresser, a schoolmaster and a student. One of the wardens at another post had a title and his butler used to bring his master's sandwiches on a silver platter!

RESCUE SERVICES

It was the rescue services who had the responsibility of locating and then rescuing those buried under the rubble of a bombed or damaged building. It was also their task to remove corpses. As these brave men clambered about among the masonry, other services, such as first aid, fire and ambulance staff, the WVS (Women's Volunteer Service) and concerned neighbours would be near by ready to help.

The air-raid damage shown here might be anywhere; in fact it is in Hendon and was caused by a V2 rocket. The entrance to the underground shelter shows how safe such refuges could be. The need for heavy lifting gear and rescue personnel trained in its use is obvious.

The rescue services were staffed by men who were knowledgeable about the building trade. At first there were two sorts, heavy and light rescue squads, but these were amalgamated in April 1940. Each squad had a lorry containing cutting and lifting tackle, and baulks of heavy timber for shoring up buildings. The squad consisted of one leader, three skilled men and six men. The squads were based with other services, at such places as the council depots in Squires Lane, Woodhouse Road, Chesterfield Road, Friern Barnet Council yard and East Barnet sewage works in Osidge Lane. Most councils simply transferred their own workers but Barnet and Finchley used local builders as well on an ad hoc basis.

Although they were experienced, rescue personnel were still sent on training courses where they were taught some of the practical skills required, as this timetable from Hendon shows:

HENDON RESCUE SERVICES TRAINING SCHEDULE – DAY THREE

8.15 hours	Lecture
	Use of starting and follow up wedges, jacks and packings, cranes, derricks, sheer legs and other lifting tackle
9.00	Practice session
	Handling heavy timbers, clearance of debris, holding up floors

13.15	Lecture	
	Rescue parties – their equipment and work	
	Recovery of dead bodies. Rescue of trapped or injured persons	
14.30	Practice of above	
	This to be carried out in full anti-gas clothing	
16.50	Examination (written and practical)	
19.00	Course closes	

They were to learn more from bitter experience, however, including the importance of carrying a water bottle, since people buried in a building were frequently half-choked by dust in the nose and mouth.

After an incident, rescue workers demolished dangerous buildings, helped people retrieve their belongings, put any usable building materials aside for reuse and helped salvage furniture that had not been destroyed. One of their important spare-time activities was reglazing shattered windows.

There were three categories of damaged buildings: category A comprised buildings needing immediate demolition; category B were those not repairable in under 1,800 man hours and therefore were to be demolished; and category C were houses capable of being repaired.

In February 1941 Finchley Council were told by their borough surveyor:

Owing to the recent lull in enemy activity, I have been able to collate some statistics for the period 31/8/40 to 31/1/41 (that is for the first five months of the Blitz):

Total number of	damaged premises	6,082
	premises repaired	3,937
	orders issued to builders	3,587
Inspections made by borough staff		over 10,000
'Lots' of furniture	salvaged	362
ditto	and stored	78
ditto	conveyed to other places	13
Number of sites	needing clearance	172
ditto	already cleared	40
ditto	in hand	34

23 Council employees plus outside contractors as required are out into this work. Building materials, particularly large pieces of timber, are salvaged whenever possible.

Number of houses requisitioned 250 including 50 as a reserve.

Nothing was wasted as this excerpt from the 'For Sale' columns of the *Finchley Press* of February 1941 shows: 'Cheap firewood. Unusable timber from demolished houses. One shilling per cwt. Phone . . .'

Public air-raid shelters like this one in Brunswick Park usually accommodated about 100 people though others were larger. They were organized by shelter marshals. Toilet facilities were primitive. Shelters like these would protect those inside against flying debris, but would not withstand a direct hit.

CASUALTY SERVICES

If the rescue services had the grimmest task, the various medical services cannot have been far behind. It was the task of the duty doctor at the control centre, working on the information supplied by the wardens, to allocate and plan the medical response.

The first link in this chain was the mobile first-aid parties located at various depots. They worked in teams of four men and a driver, all trained in first aid; many were members of the Red Cross or St John organizations. Their first task was to help rescue teams and decide medical priorities – severe cases to hospital, less severe to the nearest first-aid posts and those uninjured to a rest centre or a quick return home. At a later date, incident doctors joined the teams to provide an on-the-spot diagnosis and treatment.

As well as the conventional ambulances, there were fleets of auxiliary ambulances, mostly converted vans and usually driven by women. It was their task to get the vehicle through, no matter what the hazards: falling bombs, debris strewn across the road, craters and fires. Once there, the job was not over. There were long waits at the incident as well as the trauma of dealing with appalling injuries.

The first-aid posts were the second link. They were staffed by a doctor, one trained nurse and a number of nurses and auxiliaries. Friern Barnet's posts, for example, included Oakleigh Infants School in Oakleigh Road North, the Church Hall in Friern Barnet Lane, Holly Park Infants School, and the Palmsville Garage in Colney Hatch Lane.

By 1940 Friern Barnet had two mobile first-aid posts, which included stretcher bearers in their crews. Finchley had twenty-four private cars for 'walking wounded'.

For an example of how the various services combined, see pp. 48–50.

HOSPITALS

A number of hospitals served the area and dealt with casualties sent on by first-aid parties and others. They included Colney Hatch Hospital, Finchley Memorial Hospital, Wellhouse Hospital, Victoria Cottage Hospital, Colindale Hospital (LCC), Redhill Hospital and Manor Cottage Hospital.

In 1946 Finchley Memorial Hospital published a small booklet entitled *Your Hospital in War*. It is a remarkable and moving work, all the better for having been written soon after the events. We know of no other account which matches it as a record of the suffering of those Finchley citizens injured in air raids and the dedication of those whose duty it was to care for them. Let the following extracts stand as a record and a tribute to all Barnet's hospitals.

From as early as September 1938 the hospital was busy with its preparations for war:

> The so-called 'Munich' crisis of Sept 1938 awoke in many of us the stark realisation that war was coming. This was reinforced by the issue of gas-masks and the digging of trenches in our open space by the main road.
>
> The Medical Staff . . . called emergency meetings . . . They formed 'teams' and assigned duties. They developed study groups in which they pooled their individual experiences of military surgery in the Great War (1914–1918) . . . As a result, each surgeon . . . possessed a folio of typed articles covering the science and art of military surgery up to date.

The auxiliary and other services were organized and trained:

> . . . blood transfusion would be an integral part of the Hospital's treatment of Air Raid casualties . . . an appeal was broadcast for blood donors. Finchley's generous response resulted in 150 donors being tested, grouped and a rota formed. When air raid casualties were admitted, the excellence of planning and training in the blood transfusion department was amply demonstrated.
>
> . . . The possibility of attack by gas was a serious pre-occupation. . . . a special department for the reception of wounded who had also been gassed was built . . . with the great help of the 'Gas Officer for Finchley', teams were trained for this exacting work.
>
> The uniform of the Red Cross nurse was soon to be a welcome sight in every

department of the Hospital's work. We cannot say more than that they lived up to their emblem and the reputation of their famous Society.

By telephone or messenger [the control officer] is the co-ordinating link between the hospital and all the outside services which deal with air raids . . . This onerous and responsible work, which included regular 'all night' duty, was undertaken and carried through by a rota of faithful volunteers.

By the declaration of war, all was ready:

1939, September 3 . . . the voice of the Prime Minister declaring war on Germany. Our scouts and helpers paused for a few minutes from the hard work of filling sandbags and erecting barricades. Within the hospital, the beds stood in rows, vacant and ready. All our equipment was distributed, laid out and for immediate use. We were ready for action. We had been appointed the Casualty Receiving Hospital for Finchley and Friern Barnet. That duty was assigned to us within the 'Bart's' Sector of the Emergency Medical service of which we formed part. Our Section Officer was the late Sir Girling Ball of Bart's who was moving into his new quarters at Mill Hill School, now in the process of being transformed into a hospital.

At this time, we expected hundreds of casualties from immediate air attacks. It is hard to recall the deep feelings of tension which pervaded us all. But we were to wait another year for the attacks to come . . .

We developed a coloured card system (a relic of field ambulance days). These . . . resembled large luggage labels and were tied to the patient. A *red* card indicated operation as soon as possible. A *blue* card denoted resuscitation to be urgent. A *yellow* card was to be for a gas case, and so on.

We pushed small opaque objects into a loaf of bread and then located them by X-rays . . . Then we 'operated' on our loaves and found our objects, as we were later to find bomb fragments in the living subject by the same method. We held air raid practices along with members of the Aid Posts and Ambulance Services . . . The 'Wounded', I think, were glad to escape from our hands!

In July and August 1940 the Battle of Britain swept the Germans from the daylight skies. The nights, however, were still full of action:

1940, September 22. To-night there are more bombs and incendiaries. And now our Hospital goes 'into action' – the real thing for the first time. We had ten immediate admissions, all wounded, eight of them severely. We had our first sight of war on children.

A little boy of 9 had his left leg nearly blown off where it joins the body and the main artery was severed. There he lay, covered in grime and dirt, pale and pulseless, almost lifeless, faintly breathing. A nurse sat beside him, holding him. The writer, well accustomed to the human debris of a battlefield, will never forget the surge of pity and anger caused by the sight of that little lad. We were to see such a sight again and again, but never to grow used to it.

Now it was to be air attack night after night for many nights, and Finchley seldom escaped some bombing. The Hospital had to be constantly 'on its toes' and it was frequently stretched to its capacity. It admitted casualties sometimes nightly. All nights were tense and noisy, giving little chance of recuperative sleep for an exhausted staff and their helpers.

Until the month of December, it was a common occurrence for the Hospital to be hard at work all night . . . it became necessary to call upon an increasing number of its 'off duty' staff. (As a routine, two doctors, in addition to the Resident Medical Officer, slept in the Hospital each night.)

Our climax was on the night of November 15th, the night of land mines in High Road, East Finchley, and in Ossulton Way. That night we had by ambulance twenty-seven casualties, and we gave shelter to others who were shaken and homeless. On that occasion, some worked for fourteen hours and more at a stretch, and the whole nursing staff of the Hospital must have been 'on duty'. Our nurses were splendid and, without exception, all could be relied upon.

The Finchley Hospital prided itself upon its 'anti-shock' measures:

Its blood transfusion service was a purely local voluntary effort, organised on our own initiative, without suggestion from any other quarter. In turn, two of our admirable blood donors slept in the Hospital each night, ready to give a pint of blood at a moment's notice. Additional donors were brought from their homes and 'shelters' through 'the blitz' as required. Stored blood has been, of necessity and for good reason, much relied upon. We believed that 'fresh' blood had a special virtue. When we were congratulated in the Sector upon our excellent resuscitation, we felt that the praise was due to our blood donors, who had spent many nights away from homes they were loath to leave, or had braved 'the blitz' to come to us.

By the end of November, our records showed that we had admitted a hundred severe casualties, sent to us for hospital treatment by the Aid Post and Ambulance Service. Of that total, only five died, and these within a few hours of admission. There were no other deaths. We are proud of this record.

The X-ray department functioned at all hours throughout the Blitz:

It is a pleasure to record the keenness and sense of duty of our Radiographer, who was always willing to come to the Hospital through the thick of it. We shall not forget a particular chest case on our first night in action (one always remembers first nights), when we watched through the X-ray screen a bomb fragment at the back of the heart, moving to and fro with its every beat. This case we transferred the following day in good condition, with another like it, to the Chest Centre of our base hospital, 'Bart's,' which had moved to Hill End, St. Albans. That afternoon, we motored out and witnessed the skill with which the bomb fragments were removed. Both patients made complete recoveries.

As so often in war, scientific advances were made of necessity. Finchley Hospital experimented successfully with the treatment of war wounds:

From our experience and study of past wars . . . we proposed to add experimentally the local use in the wound of the new sulphonamide drugs, popularly known as M. & B. Already in our work, we had crushed some of the sulphonamide tablets intended to be taken by mouth, and dusted the powder into wounds caused by street accidents. The result was encouraging.

In a lecture at the Hammersmith Post-Graduate Medical School on August 11th, 1940, it was stated that there had been studies in America on the use of sulphonamide crystals or powder in the wounds of compound fractures of the bones, with good results reported, but that the treatment was still experimental. On the night of September 22nd, all our injured had their wounds treated by this method. After as complete a removal as possible from the wound of all damaged tissue and foreign material, the M. & B. powder was dusted and pressed into every part of it. A light internal dressing was applied and free drainage secured. Other acknowledged surgical principles were followed. The results exceeded our expectations. Our patients were comfortable and without fever or inflammation and free from pain. In many cases, re-dressings after operation were not required for several weeks . . . (The method rapidly became the standard one in all theatres of war.)

The drama of a casualty hospital at work during an air attack is vividly conveyed:

The sirens have sounded the familiar 'alert'. The Hospital 'stands by'. The Control Officers go their rounds of inspection; the firemen man the pumps; the fire-watchers are at their stations. The Rover Scouts are here in strength (and strength will probably be needed before the night is over) for stretcher-bearing, lifting and carrying, putting up and moving beds, helping with the heavy and rough work, taking messages – the handymen of the whole show. The Red Cross nurses move quietly about among the nursing staff. The doctors on duty make their survey. The blood donors have arrived. The cars stand ready outside. The operating theatre staff are sterilising the instruments. In the dimmed-out wards patients try to sleep. Are we to have 'a packet' to-night, or will it be for someone else?

Hullo! that was a near one!

Almost immediately the telephone rings. The Control Officer passes on the word that 'an incident' has occurred and casualties may be expected. The first ambulance will arrive almost immediately.

What does it hold of living or dead? What remnants are within of what was a happy home but a few minutes ago?

The ambulance gong sounds and the casualty entrance doors are opened. The dimly lit reception hall is behind and the 'black-out' is all around. In the sky, there are the searchlights, we see the shell-bursts, the air is full of the sound of planes and explosions. Our young Scouts, the stretcher-bearers, by the light of dimmed torches, carry in the wounded and the dead. Rapidly the Medical Officers 'sort out' and 'size up' their cases. What is immediate, such as haemorrhage, is attended to at once, but much more will have to be done later, for these patients come from a collapsed building, and lime and dust and plaster and mortar cover and permeate them. Clothing, hair, ears, eyes, nose are full of

the mixture, and so are the wounds! The patient is in a state of shock. His life
hangs on a thread. Until shock is countered, even taking his boots off may turn
the scale against him. And so with a 'blue card' attached, and perhaps a 'red
card' to follow, he is moved into the ward. The Resuscitation Medical Officer is
already 'grouping' his blood, and the first blood donor of the night has given 'a
pint of his best.' The nurse has given the morphia ordered and the warm
electric cradles are over the patient. The night's work has begun, and with the
arrival of a second and third ambulance, it will go on hour after hour –
reception room to ward for resuscitation – ward to X-ray room – X-ray room to
operating theatre – theatre to ward again.

The 'all clear' sounds at dawn, but the work for the injured goes on until
everything has been done for all.

MORTUARIES

Local undertakers and hospitals were generally able to cope with the number of
corpses, but the authorities had prepared for deaths on the vast scale suggested by
the Committee for Imperial Defence. On the first day of the war, therefore, the
Mill Hill dustbin lorry was ordered to stand by at the depot ready to carry corpses
to the mortuary.

Finchley built three extra mortuaries, at St Barnabas' Hall, Gainsborough
Road, N12; at St Luke's Hall, N3; and at the Methodist Hall, Park Road, N2 (for
fifty bodies). In addition there was already a municipal mortuary behind the fire
station on the North Circular Road. Those for East Barnet were at 5 Station Road
and 1 Lyonsdown Road (the latter cost £150).

Temporary mortuaries for the northern area were built in Bethune Park and on
the Colney Hatch Lane allotments. There was another in Mays Lane, Barnet, and
for a short time one at the South Herts Golf Club in Totteridge Lane.

Part-time staff were recruited from local undertakers, who provided their own
vans. Friern Barnet bought a second-hand mortuary van for £400. Not to be
outdone, Barnet bought a brand new van with a zinc lined body for easy cleaning
for £1,000. Finchley used the van of Gentry, a local baker, as a temporary hearse,
though presumably Gentry's customers were not told.

In October 1942 Hendon Council had all its assets listed for insurance purposes.
The Hendon mortuary, situated at the rear of the town hall, had these furnishings:

Oak mortuary table	value £25	0s	0d
1 pair oak trestles	£4	0s	0d
Oak table with twisted legs	£21	0s	0d
3 bentwood chairs	£2	5s	0d
Set of scales and weights	£4	0s	9d
2 sets mortuary surgical instruments	£10	10s	0d
White painted sloping top desk	£2	0s	0d
with 2 drawers on square legs			
White painted waste bin	£1	0s	0d
Light fittings and bulbs throughout	£15	10s	0d

Each mortuary had a doctor on call, a superintendent, four staff as required and a full-time caretaker. All had a telephone installed. Records were kept using form CWD One (Civilian War Dead One). Copies were sent to the local town hall and to the police. The mortuary superintendent also had to report any case of suspicious death. There were rooms for identified and unidentified bodies. At Finchley, the bodies were placed in a hessian shroud, though Friern Barnet used cardboard coffins. Impervious thick rubber coffins were also available. Barnet had a roll of canvas 250 ft long, which was cut up as required, and effects were kept in labelled canvas bags.

The temporary mortuaries were rarely used.

GAS

The horrific gas casualties of the First World War were fresh in the mind in 1939. There were three groups of gas: poison gas, tear gas and blister gas. Protection against poison and tear gases was provided by a gas mask, although there is some

Wearing a gas mask was a frightening experience for young children. Rehearsals like the one shown here were frequent and intended to familiarize children with the mask. The photograph is one of an official series.

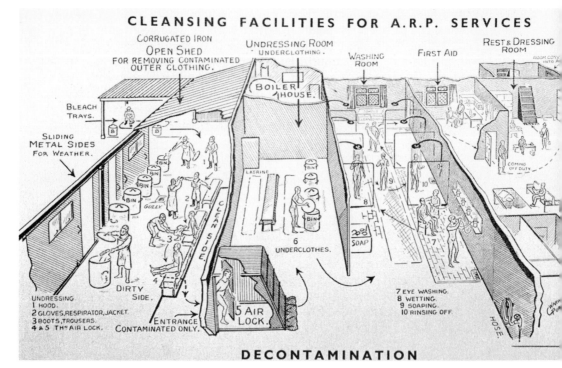

CLEANSING FACILITIES FOR A.R.P. SERVICES

CORRUGATED IRON
OPEN SHED
FOR REMOVING CONTAMINATED
OUTER CLOTHING.

UNDRESSING ROOM
· UNDERCLOTHING ·

WASHING
ROOM

FIRST AID

REST & DRESSING
ROOM

BLEACH
TRAYS.

BOILER
HOUSE.

SLIDING
METAL SIDES
FOR WEATHER.

LATRINE

DIRTY
SIDE.

UNDRESSING.
1 HOOD.
2 GLOVES, RESPIRATOR, JACKET.
3 BOOTS, TROUSERS.
4 & 5 THE AIR LOCK.

5 AIR
LOCK.

ENTRANCE
CONTAMINATED ONLY.

UNDERCLOTHES.

SOAP

7 EYE WASHING.
8 WETTING.
9 SOAPING.
10 RINSING OFF.

DECONTAMINATION

Decontamination, that is the process of cleaning dangerous gases from someone's body and clothing, was carried out at special centres. This suggested layout comes from the advice given to local councils by the Home Office in 1938.

evidence that the gas masks issued would have been relatively ineffective. The problem of issuing masks to everyone in the country was enormous. Once the masks had been distributed and fitted, the wardens carried out regular checks.

Mustard and other liquid blister gases would have been dealt with by people wearing special protective clothing. The liquid was to be diluted with water to render it harmless and flushed down the sewers. Special gas decontamination chambers containing shower rooms were set up at Bethune Park, St Barnabas' Hall, the old chapel in Totteridge Lane and elsewhere, but none was ever used.

A practice at Finchley revealed that though the protective suits were hung on clothes' hangers at the depots, there was nothing to hang them on to dry at the decontamination centre. Two wire coat hangers at a halfpenny each were officially ordered and delivered!

Both the Allies and the Germans had large stocks of gases and there is no doubt that Churchill would have ordered the use of gas had the Germans invaded. Fortunately the stocks were never used. Many homes still have a gas mask somewhere in the attic.

FIRE SERVICES

The realization that the enemy would use incendiary bombs resulted in a number of decisions. In 1939 our local councils each had their own fire brigade. Finchley even upgraded one fire engine by replacing its solid tyres with pneumatic ones.

As we have seen, an auxiliary fire service had been recruiting since early 1938. But no organization, however large and well equipped, could have countered the heavy air raids that took place in the East End of London – particularly the docks. The huge conflagrations in many cases had simply to burn themselves out. As it happened, our area was not as badly affected as some and our local fire units could be called upon by other areas under a reciprocal arrangement.

In 1939 firemen were equipped with so-called 'heavy' and 'light' trailer fire pumps. These were towed to the scene of the fire by lorry or, in the case of Friern Barnet, by one of the five cars hired for the purpose. By May 1940 Friern Barnet had fifteen trailer pumps; East Barnet had a special pump capable of dealing with damaged sewers; and Hendon, being larger, had eleven heavy trailer pumps and sixty light pumps.

Auxiliary fire stations supplemented the regular stations. They included St Andrew's School, Oakleigh Park; Palmsville Garage, Colney Hatch Lane; Clockhouse Garage near Hampden Square; and Belmont in Cockfosters. Colney Hatch Hospital, the STC factory in New Southgate and the Finchley factory of Simms had their own auxiliary units.

One of the lessons learnt in the London Blitz was that damage to water mains could result in a shortage of water. This was solved by building a number of large tanks (called 'dams') each of which could hold between 5,000 and 20,000 gallons

The high risk of fire caused by German incendiary bombs was met by the distribution of trailer fire pumps. Every local council had several of these pumps stored at auxiliary fire stations at strategic points around the district.

The stirrup pump was the most widely available method of enabling house holders to tackle small fires caused by the German 2 lb incendiary bomb. Many houses had a pump and a bucket of water at the top of the stairs.

of water. They were marked EWS (Emergency Water Supply) in large letters. They proved an irresistible and dangerous attraction to young children.

Firemen's clothing needs to be especially thick to combat heat. In 1939 Friern Barnet bought 39 tunics, 74 pairs of trousers and 39 caps at a cost of £2 10s 2d (£2.51) per uniform. Special boots were also required, as well as waterproof and top coats. The traditional brass helmet, of course, had long been replaced by wooden crowns covered with leather. The steel helmets now supplied to firemen, while essential in air raids, presented the same hazard as the earlier brass ones – they could be lethal in contact with exposed electrical cables.

Possibly the most valuable lesson learnt from the heavy raids on London was that small fires, if unattended, become large ones. It was for this reason that teams of firewatchers, sometimes called fireguards, were recruited. They patrolled every street and were located in nearly every major building so that they could tackle small fires or alert the fire brigade when something more serious threatened. This began as a voluntary activity but became compulsory during 1941. By February 1945 in East Barnet, for example, the total number of registered firewatchers was 8,539 women and 8,559 men.

Among the equipment supplied to firewatchers was the famous 'stirrup pump' – a simple, hand operated and extremely robust pump which could draw water from almost any container. Some of the 20,000 or so supplied survive to this day.

In May 1941 the two branches of the fire service were combined to form the National Fire Service. Trailer fire-pumps were gradually replaced by pumps mounted on dark green lorries carrying other equipment as well, the so called 'Green Goddesses'.

There were many acts of heroism by firemen, recorded and unrecorded. It is invidious to single out any particular one. Let this following account, from the *Hendon Times*, 8 August 1941, stand for all:

> The first wartime award to a Hendon fireman will shortly be made to Sub-officer C.W. Hill, who will receive the George Medal in recognition of his work during a recent heavy raid [the George Medal, instituted on 24 September 1940, is awarded for acts of courage to civilians only].
>
> Sub-officer Hill was fighting a fire, when he was told that there were two people trapped in the basement of a building that was alight from ground to top floor. He entered the building by the ground floor passage, but was unable to advance owing to the intense heat. He then broke through the pavement light and was able to enter the basement. Although the smoke and heat were intense he was able to bring the trapped persons to a position at the front where they could be pulled to safety. During the time that this rescue was being enacted, the rest of the building collapsed. Sub-officer Hill then brought out Station Officer Morgan, who had been overcome by smoke and was pulled up on the end of a line. The London Gazette said he showed 'utter disregard of danger and displayed conspicuous courage and fortitude'.

Other Hendon residents to be awarded the George Medal in 1941 included Special Constable T. Hite, A.G. Hammon, J. Carley and E.G. Jared.

THE POLICE

In common with firemen and medical service personnel, policemen had additional war-time duties. This had been foreseen and, before the war, an auxiliary Police War Reserve had been formed which was called up when war broke out. Among its members were a number of part-time special constables.

The police worked closely with the civil defence services and frequently found themselves assisting in all the activities involved in an incident. Located above all our local police stations was the famous siren which wailed the signals for 'alert' and 'all clear'.

Other police duties included traffic control, evacuation of residents from dangerous areas, prevention of looting from bombed buildings, keeping a tally of the dead and injured and informing next of kin.

One local special constable, Jack Prime, wrote the following account of his experiences:

> In 1938, when Chamberlain came back with his famous 'piece of paper', it was said that if Britain was strong Hitler would be afraid to start a war. So people started to join and be trained as ARP wardens and so on. I knew several

The police played a vital though unspectacular role in civil defence. This official photograph was intended to show the correct way to carry the civil defence gas mask.

policemen and they persuaded me in 1938 to enlist as a War Reserve Policeman where I received training in things such as first aid. When war broke out in 1939 we were instructed to go to Barnet Police Station where we were given a number (mine was 629), a tin hat with the initials WRP on the front, an army gas mask in a haversack and wooden chair leg as a truncheon. The pay was £3 per week.

We were based at Woodside House, Baxendale's old house on the corner of Totteridge Lane. My first duty was to patrol Totteridge Lane. People came out and asked what they should do with their animals in the event of a gas attack. All we could do was to suggest that they covered the kennels and cages with wet sacks – we did not know any better than the owners.

The first months of the war were quiet but when the air raids started our job was to evacuate people away from any unexploded bombs (UXBs) and keep the traffic moving. One bomb I remember fell in Finchley Park. I was on duty when the Army dug it out and I said to one of the soldiers 'where is the bomb?' 'Here it is,' he said and hit it a great thwack with his shovel! I didn't stop to ask any more questions! Another UXB fell in Athenaeum Road. It went through the roof, the upper floors of the house and finished up at the feet of the house owner who was in his armchair sitting by his fire . . . .

I saw some terrible and gruesome things during the air raids. A parachute bomb fell in Bells Hill, Barnet. They were big bombs and did a lot of damage. I was sent there and saw an ARP warden whose job was to pick up the pieces of flesh and put them in a bucket. I saw him put in a human hand and a scalp which was too much for me. On returning to the site several days later I saw two men picking up a small body on their shovels and putting it into a sack.

The War Reserve Police had a number of duties. One of the most important was manning the blue police boxes in different parts of the district and trying to prevent the looting of bombed buildings. . . . We also guarded places of strategic importance such as telephone exchanges and checked passes. I was on duty at the telephone exchange one day when a young lad of about 12 years of age came over and talked to me. His face was very pitted and when I asked him what had happened he said it was from glass splinters when a bomb had exploded in Derwent Villas. The glass apparently worked its way out on its own and he showed me his handkerchief in which there were a dozen or so splinters of glass.

A very unusual incident was when I was asked to report to Barnet Police Station. No reason was given. When I got there I was interviewed by a Police Inspector and two other people. Apparently some man had reported that I had asked him to lend me Hitler's book 'Mein Kampf'. I knew nothing about it but the man had taken down incorrectly the policeman's number which was like mine.

Later in the war came the V1 – the buzz-bomb. The first one that came over I thought was an aeroplane. When its engine stopped, I thought it had been shot down by our guns. Soon they were coming over night and day and when that engine stopped you dived to the ground for safety. One of the worst incidents of the war was the V1 which fell about 8.30 a.m. one morning on the woodshop of the Standard Telephone factory. A number of people were killed. But the incident I shall never forget was the V1 which fell in Russell Gardens at 6.00 a.m. on Friday 13 July 1944. Twin boys living in one of the houses were killed. We were living nearby in Oakleigh Road. Our roof, doors and windows were shattered. Repair men came later to cover over the roof with large tarpaulins which were anchored by tying on to dustbins. That night, the rain came down, the wind blew and the dustbins rattled all night. The V2 rockets were another terrifying thing that had to be faced.

When that V1 dropped and damaged our house, I was taken ill with delayed shock and had several weeks recuperating in the country. I was still there when the war finished.

THE WOMEN'S VOLUNTARY SERVICE (WVS)

One of the most remarkable stories of the war is the part played by women. It is also one of the scandals that their achievements often went unrecognized and that they were often shabbily treated. In 1941 unmarried women between the ages of twenty and thirty were called up for war work in the factories or uniformed services. By 1943, 90 per cent of single women and 80 per cent of married women were in war work of some national importance with the call-up extended to single women of between nineteen and fifty-one years of age.

Many more elderly women, or younger women with children, undertook voluntary work with organizations such as the WVS. This was, of course, in addition to their family responsibilities. The range of activities carried out by the WVS was remarkable. One of their members during (and after) the war years was Olive Dyke, who recorded her memories of those times with the Friern Barnet branch of the service:

I joined the Women's Voluntary Service in February 1941. I was asked if I would take on the emergency feeding for Friern Barnet and I agreed, taking my instructions from a Mr Morris who was in the Control Centre in the town hall. The function of my unit was, when a bomb fell, to feed the people affected by the incident. To do this we had a number of feeding centres located in various

WVS Centres, such as this one in Friern Barnet, carried stocks of tinned food to meet the many wartime emergencies. Among the regulations was one requiring that the tins should be inverted every week.

parts of the area. The centres housed stocks of tinned food and were staffed by a WVS team working on a rota basis – the idea being that the team nearest to the incident would be called out. To do the job of cooking, they were supported by a Mobile Emergency Feeding Unit (MEFU) whose equipment was housed in the Advance Laundry in the High Road, Finchley. This comprised sheets of corrugated iron to make a kind of portable shed which could be quickly erected, and a number of mobile wood-fired boilers on which the cooking was done.

The WVS, of course, did many different tasks during the war. An important part of our work was looking after the Repair Party canteens. When a bomb dropped, lots of men from the council and local builders were called to the site to undertake repairs. They had to be catered for with light refreshments such as tea, coffee, rolls and cakes, and to do this a canteen would be set up near the incident, usually in a nearby damaged building which might have to be made safe for us to work in. Tinned goods were supplied by the government and our canteen was a centre where the men could be found. We made 'a good cup of tea' and I remember even today that one pint of milk was used for twenty-five cups. We also had a mobile canteen which visited bombed sites.

We also played a big part in the Holidays at Home scheme. This was designed to encourage people to take their holidays at home rather than going away and using valuable transport and resources. . . . Another activity I helped in were the various National Savings weeks. These had titles such as 'Wings for Victory' Week and each area had a savings target. If you reached the target you were given a flag to fly. Councillor Foley was chairman of the Savings Committee and artists such as Cyril Fletcher and Betty Astell gave concerts in support of the activity. We sold savings stamps and certificates in one of the local electricity showrooms.

A more unusual service during wartime was the collection of food scraps for pig food. A number of dustbins were located in various streets into which the local residents put their scraps and these were collected regularly by us for converting into 'cakes' for local pigs. A section leader of the WVS was also responsible for running the so-called British Restaurants which would supply a good quality lunch for around 6d.

My voluntary work was seven days a week. The canteen opened at 9.30 a.m. and closed about 4.00 p.m. I made many friends in my work and felt that what I was doing made a real contribution to the war effort. There was a wonderful spirit among the people I worked with and the WVS *never* let anyone down. The war brought people together and you made lots of friends.

THE HOME GUARD

By June 1940, after the evacuation at Dunkirk, the British Army had left in France thousands of tons of equipment, stores and ammunition, and invasion seemed imminent.

A War Office document dated 8 June gives the armament available to defend the entire British Isles as follows:

2 pounder anti tank guns	54
Bren guns with 1,200 rounds each	2,300
2 in and 3 in mortars	very few
Armoured cars (mainland)	37
(Ireland)	15
Light tanks	395
Medium tanks	72
Heavy tanks	33
Field guns (with 200 rounds per gun)	420
Medium and heavy guns (with 150 rounds per gun)	163

There were also fifty-seven coastal defence batteries with two Victorian guns in each.

This does not represent only those armaments standing in reserve at depots; these were all the weapons available anywhere to resist an impending invasion by a German army not only well equipped but rearmed with vast quantities of captured British war material.

'We expect to be attacked here ourselves, both from the air (by bombing) and by parachute and airborne troops in the near future, and are getting ready for them,' wrote Churchill to Roosevelt on 15 May. Churchill's idea was to form the Local Defence Volunteers. This was announced by Anthony Eden on 14 May 1940. The response was immediate. Within six days more than a quarter of a million men had been enrolled and by August the Home Guard (as the LDV was now called) had a strength of more than a million.

There were few uniforms at first, and denims were issued. Battle dress arrived gradually, so that by 25 November 1940 an order was issued withdrawing denims. November also saw the first issue of steel helmets and boots, though there was a shortage of the more popular sizes. Socks were never issued. At the 'Stand Down' parade of May 1945, the commanding officer made the point that he had 7,000 armed men on parade all wearing civilian socks.

One important factor about the Home Guard – though often overlooked – is that by undertaking static guard duty they released the regular army for training for the invasion of Europe. When the Normandy landings took place in June 1944, the Home Guard was mobilized to deal with a possible German counter-invasion.

On 3 August 1940 Home Guard units were formally affiliated to their county regiments and wore their badges. The local unit was the 24th Battalion of the Middlesex Regiment. Local companies were the No. 11, drawn from East and Friern Barnet, North Finchley and Totteridge, and No. 12 from Finchley and Hendon. A particularly interesting unit was the 46th County of London Battalion formed from London Transport staff and based at Finchley bus garage. It was formed on 1 February 1941, and its first commanding officer was Lieutenant-Colonel A.J. Croucher.

W.J. Allibone, who served in the Barnet detachment, wrote 'Not all the Home Guard were volunteers. Harold Eastwood and I were conscripted because we were engaged on essential war work and therefore in a reserved occupation.' Training took place whenever members could be spared, mostly in the summer evenings and at weekends. The legend that pikes were the only weapons available is unfortunately not true. Six-foot lengths of gas piping with a knife jammed in were not issued until June 1941 and even then stayed in the storeroom as nobody could work out how to hold a pike and fire a machine gun simultaneously.

The first volunteers were men of maturer years, many of whom had fought in the First World War. 'Dad's Army' they certainly were not, and gave good accounts of themselves in mock battles and exercises against the regular army. Later on in the war, young men of about seventeen joined up for some kind of pre-service training.

It is sad to record that one of their first duties in this district was to provide guards for bombed properties in Woodside Park to prevent looters. Other duties included guarding railway tunnels.

Doug Austin recalls what life was like in the Home Guard:

Returning from work, I used to have a quick meal (spam or Woolton pie) and then don my well-fitting denim uniform (trousers up to the armpits, and the blouse came down below the wrist and waist), together with civilian shoes and an armband with the letters LDV on it. About 6.30 p.m. we, that is a motley band of clerks, dustmen, unemployed bank managers, retired army officers, etc., assembled at HQ, which was an ordinary semi-detached house. Training was a mixture of lectures and arms drill.

After the name was changed to the Home Guard, we became more like real soldiers. We had serge khaki battle dress, a forage cap, webbing equipment, a gas cape, a tin hat with the Middlesex Regiment badge on it and real army boots and gaiters. Each one of us also had a real rifle and bayonet. There was also an issue of one Lewis gun for about every thirty men.

Sunday morning parades were compulsory. We crawled about in mock battles or went on route marches to show the local population that we were ready for anything – well almost. The marches were great fun: one private used to bring his dog along as a mascot.

Other activities included a weekend of battlecraft at an army camp. We fired our rifles at a range near Mill Hill barracks. We also learned how to throw the 36 grenade. Our bomb corporal sat in a sandbagged shelter supervising us as we placed the fuse in the grenade. He became steadily paler as the day went on.

We were only called out once and that was a false alarm. During the 'doodlebug' era we had to do fire-watching at HQ but again nothing actually happened.

The social life was great. Our second HQ was the local pub. All rank was abandoned once we were off duty. . . . In spite of an alleged beer shortage, there was always a pint for the Home Guard.

Equipment arrived steadily, in part from the USA. The Finchley Company included an anti-tank platoon armed with anti-tank guns and Spigot mortars. The machine gun section had the ubiquitous Bren gun and the Vickers and Browning heavy machine gun. Rifle platoons had rifles, Sten guns, a few Tommy

The Simms factory Home Guard unit, c. 1944.

guns (for about six months in 1941) and grenades of various kinds. According to the Home Guard training manual, the initial issue was of British .303 Lee Enfield rifles, which were soon replaced by American Springfields, American .300 rifles, the Browning automatic rifle and the Canadian Ross rifle, which had an ear-splitting bang. All these weapons had a two-inch wide red band painted on them to indicate that they did not take standard British ammunition. By May 1941 stocks of ammunition had increased to such an extent that each man was able to fire five practice rounds.

There was a signals section equipped with flags, field lamps and wireless sets, which seemed always to go wrong or out of frequency just when they were most needed. The despatch riders rode Ariel and BSA motor bicycles painted khaki.

No. 11 Company had the use of one Crusader tank and one Churchill tank, both of which were driven by members of the company.

Simms Motor Units factory at Finchley had its own unit for factory protection as did the Standard Telephones and Cables Co. (see chapter four). The Simms unit was 63 Company of the 24th Battalion, the Middlesex Regiment.

In the event of an invasion, the duties of the Home Guard were:–

a) The disruption of petrol supplies to the enemy
b) Maintain road blocks

c) Maintain observation posts
d) Act as communication personnel and provide local guides to troops
e) Assist Police and civil authorities
f) Maintain defence posts
g) Maintain dumps for tools, wire etc
h) Store and guard arms and ammunition
i) Provision of an identification system at central and outer anti-tank lines
j) Laying of minefields

Orders said 'The general plan is that there will be NO WITHDRAWAL.' The task is:–

1) To defend to the last man and to the last round or bomb.
2) To keep open vital routes.

Military requirements will take precedence over all other requirements. Anyone disobeying an order from the military is liable to be shot.

The 'London Attack' signal will be the blowing of a steady note on sirens for five whole minutes. The anti-tank lines will then be closed except for the green road gaps.

The defences around London included the central anti-tank line (there were others in Hertfordshire and Essex) which was stated to run from the junction of the Edgware Road with Garratt Road roughly east along the north side of the LNER railway embankment to Mill Hill East Station, then north taking in Mill Hill Barracks to Totteridge Park and on round Barnet to Hadley Woods and Trent Park, using the trees as cover. The inner anti-tank line ran from Staples Corner roughly east along the North Circular Road to Southgate, using the River Brent and Strawberry Brook as partial cover.

THREE

Incident!

The use of the word 'incident' to describe the destruction of life and property by enemy action is typical of the best traditions of British understatement. In the early days of the war, the Germans dropped high-explosive bombs of varying sizes and incendiary bombs which usually weighed about a kilo. Later 'refinements' included naval mines, often attached to a parachute, and oil and

Bomb damage in Osidge Lane, 1944. The crater was said to be big enough to take a double-decker bus. When not otherwise employed, members of local rescue squads spent many hours re-glazing broken windows.

phosphorus bombs both of which caused serious fires. In the last two years of the war Germany launched its V1 and V2 rockets against Britain.

HIGH-EXPLOSIVE BOMBS

The Germans used four main sizes of high-explosive bomb: 100 kg, 250 kg, 500 kg and 1,000 kg (2,205 lb or about 1 ton). The damage caused by a bomb varied with its weight and the nature of the target. A 100 kg bomb would cause severe damage to several houses. The 1 ton bomb could destroy a whole street and make hundreds more houses uninhabitable by breaking windows and stripping off roof tiles over a wide area.

The drama of a typical 'incident' can easily be recreated by the following series of messages received by the Finchley control centre on 9 and 10 October 1940:

9/Oct/1940
20.08 hrs – Warden Post 39 to Finchley Control:
    High Road N12 between Britannia Rd & Derwent Cresc. – 2 HE. Fire & casualties, house in danger of collapse, several more houses extremely damaged, gas escaping, main road strewn with glass & debris.
20.09 – Call out Fire, rescue, first aid
20.15 – 1 × Fire pump, 1 × light rescue party, 2 stretcher parties arrived

This office block occupies 962 High Road N12, the site of the bomb incident in North Finchley of October 1940 (see above).

20.16 – London Transport, Gas, Water & Elec informed by control
20.46 – 1 × ambulance arrived
20.50 – 1 × car with sitting wounded left site
21.24 – 1 × mortuary van required
22.48 – 5 people require attention, sent to East Barnet by sitting car. One house uninhabitable at present
23.05 – Additional mortuary van required
23.21 – 2 further stretcher parties required.
23.30 – No further known casualties. Rescue party returned to depot. Of 11 casualties, 9 released, 2 dead.

10/Oct/1940
06.45 – Whetstone Police want further details regarding casualties at Derwent Cresc.
09.44 – Rescue party reports one further body recovered from 962 High Rd N20. Request mortuary van.
13.57 – Military also took casualties to hospital but did not tell rescue squad.
15.24 – Fatal: Mrs Storey; Mr Ship; Miss Ship; Mr Duncan, 962 High Rd
15.49 – Taken to hospital by military:
Mrs Falkner & Graham Falkner – detained
Mr Falkner; Mr Chisman not detained
16.08 – 11 Derwent Cresc. evacuated to Highwood Ave reception centre. Police taking charge of property. Incident now closed.
18.52 – All casualties removed. Four dead at mortuary, rest evacuated.
18.57 – Rescue party signed off at depot.

An incident that occurred on 6 January 1941 is described in much greater detail in the *Barnet Press* of 11 January:

BUNGALOWS DEMOLISHED
SEVEN KILLED BY HEAVY BOMB: REMARKABLE ESCAPES

A bomb of heavy calibre which fell on some bungalows in Barnet High Road on Sunday night completely demolished three bungalows and caused the deaths of four men, two women and a baby, all of whom were in the bungalows.

A number of other bungalows in the same road and the houses on rising ground in the roads adjoining were also damaged. Over 20 persons were injured, many of them receiving treatment in hospital and at first-aid posts. Survivors say that the noise of a bomb coming down was like the roar of an express train.

Within a few minutes of the bomb falling, rescue parties were in attendance. Their efforts were hampered by the enormous crater and the large lumps of clay that were thrown onto the wrecked buildings.

Within a few minutes, however, three of the injured, Special Police Sergeant Bolton and his wife and baby, had been released from the wreckage of their home and taken to hospital. Mr and Mrs Bolton's six-year-old daughter, however, was still buried and digging operations were continued throughout

Bomb disposal. This 100 kg (225 lb) unexploded bomb was recovered from the factory of Duple Bodies and Motors Ltd of Hendon on 6 December 1944. Although the Army dealt with most unexploded bombs, in Barnet the local fire brigade was paid 35s (£1.75) for each unexploded bomb recovered, to be divided among the five-man crew.

the night and for several more days. The body still had not been found on Thursday, when we went to press.

Mr Cyril Barnard, who was one of the people who lost their lives, had suffered from bombing on the south coast, where he had previously lived, and had recently lost his office in London. He was the organiser for fire-watching for the road and was due to go on duty later the same night. His father and mother, Mr and Mrs Barnard, and his sister were killed in the same bungalow. In the next bungalow, Mr Ernest Howell lost his life, but his wife was rescued and taken to hospital. Next door again, Mr and Mrs Herbert Barker were both killed.

One of the most remarkable escapes among the many which people nearby had was that of Mr A. Wilson, director of a garage, who was driving along the road when the bomb fell. 'I didn't hear a thing,' said Mr Wilson, 'although the car was cruising down the hill in neutral. Suddenly there was a tremendous flash and the car was hurled round in the road and debris crashed through the roof onto the back seats. Fortunately there was no one there. I pulled up at once, switched off the engine, and at that moment a man came running out of a house nearby crying "Help. Help!" I ran back with him and helped him release his little son from his bed on which huge lumps of clay had crashed, burying him. After seeing them alright, I ran across the road where I could see mounds of earth and wreckage. By that time there were crowds of people about and I went with some of them into the remains of a bungalow. We saw a woman caught in the debris with only a face showing. She was dead. A man, who had been crushed, was caught by the leg. It was a terrible moment.

'After seeing that the rescue workers had all the assistance that they wanted, I drove off in the remains of my car. The whole of one side of the car was crushed in, all but two windows were smashed and one mudguard has not been found since. When I look at the car, I realise more and more how lucky I was, but honestly I felt and saw very little. The back seats were covered with clay and bricks.'

The man to whose aid Mr Wilson went was Mr Cullender, who, with his wife, parents and seven-year-old son were all in the front room of their bungalow. 'I didn't hear the bomb,' said Mr Cullender, 'but before it fell there had been heavy gunfire, and I saw my boy come towards me on the bed. I leaned towards him and at the same moment, the bomb fell and huge pieces of clay crashed through the roof and ceiling, landing on the boy's bed. The others were alright, although practically all the ceiling, rafters and tiles crashed through the hole. The bed on which Derek was lying was crushed and he was pinned down by clay and debris.' Mr Cullender and his father were unable to move the clay but with Mr Wilson's assistance they were able to do so and managed to free the boy and fling the clay through the window. Derek suffered from shock but was otherwise unhurt.

Mr H. Miller and his wife, whose home was badly damaged when a boulder of clay crashed on the kitchen and destroyed it, are congratulating themselves on the fact that Mrs Miller delayed going into the kitchen in order to finish a row of knitting. This undoubtedly saved her life.

Mr Miller told a reporter that he was about to go out fire-watching and Mr Barnard, who was killed, was due to relieve him later in the evening. 'I asked my wife to make me a cup of coffee before I went out and she replied "I'll just finish this row of knitting first."' She had just finished the row as the bomb came down.

From everyone concerned came tributes to the efficiency of the work of the ARP personnel. They were greatly assisted in their efforts by the district householders' register, containing details of how many people usually sleep in the house, and where they usually sleep. Next of kin are also entered. One request is made in the light of experience, which is that householders should inform the Wardens of changes so that the register can be kept up to date. In this case, a search was made for somebody who had moved to the Midlands some months ago.

The bomb caused dislocation to public utility services but repair parties were soon at work.

Many more acts of heroism are recorded. Peggy Stanley, aged twenty, was visiting friends in West Hendon in February 1941 when she was caught up in an air raid.

Hendon's worst incident of the war occurred on 13 February 1941 when a 1,000 kg German bomb caused major damage to Ramsey, Ravenstone, York and Argyle Roads. Eighty people were killed and forty houses totally destroyed.

The house was wrecked by a bomb, but Miss Stanley held up the debris with her back, thereby preventing it from burying those with her. Next morning Miss Stanley went to work as usual and when she came home she set to work helping to clear up the mess.

The Hendon Council minutes, 22 February 1941, record that 'As a tribute to the memory of the victims in this tragic occurrence and as an expression of the sympathy of the whole community, the Council stood for a few moments in silence.'

Life as well as death came out of the air raids, as this report from the *Hendon Times* of February 1941 amusingly describes:

BABY BORN IN AIR RAID SHELTER

Mr and Mrs Cook live in an upstairs flat at 148 Rushgrove Avenue, Colindale. Knowing it is dangerous upstairs, they turned their Anderson shelter into a maternity ward. The walls and roof were painted light colours inside and there was electric light and electric heating. There was also an air-conditioning plant adapted from an old vacuum cleaner. When their baby came, they simply moved into the garden.

Anderson shelters were widely distributed to those with a garden in which to put one (though there is at least one recorded instance of a shelter being used indoors). Their main drawback was a tendency to flood during wet weather, and because they had no heating, they were very cold. They would have given protection against falling debris but not against a direct hit.

The only attendance on the mother was the local midwife. While being interviewed by our reporter, Mrs Cook sat in the bunk eating pears. There was just room for the baby's cot between the bunks. She said she would call the 6½ pound baby Robert Oliver, though people had suggested calling him Anderson.

It is interesting to note that an attempt was made to deceive the Germans by a dummy airfield just outside Barnet. The site was in the fields immediately south of Knightlands Farm and just west of the St Albans Road, roughly where the new golf course now is. It consisted of the fuselages of about half a dozen Hurricanes mounted on wheels and with the engines removed. A detachment of airmen moved them about the field periodically and at night rode bicycles fitted with lights round the field to imitate aircraft movements. The inhabitants of the Byng Road estate used to watch out of their bedroom windows. It is not known how successful the deception was, but bombs certainly fell on the nearby Wrotham Park estate.

MINES

Both the Allies and the Germans used mines, which are large metal balls containing about a ton of explosive. They were used mainly at sea, but a few were

Damage caused by the land mine which fell on Oakmere, an old people's home in Bell's Hill, Barnet, on 6 November 1940. Seventeen people were killed and thirty-one injured, including several nurses.

dropped over land. Parachutes were attached so that the mine casing did not break up on impact. The devastation caused by such a large amount of explosive was considerable.

Tom Page, of Barnet Road, Arkley, remembers the night of 6 November 1940, when a parachute mine landed on Oakmere, an old people's residential home in Bell's Hill, Barnet:

I was serving with the British Army and was home on a seven-day embarkation leave, prior to being shipped out to the Far East. In fact it was the last night of my leave.

My parents lived at No. 79 Wood Street, which was by the bend in the road at the top of Bells Hill, approximately 150 yards from where the mine fell. I went across to the Lord Nelson public house in West End Lane at about 8.00 in the evening to have a farewell drink with my friends. The blitzkreig was on at that time, and a heavy air raid was going on, mostly towards Central London.

Some of the people in the bar were off-duty nurses from Oakmere, whom I had got to know during my leave. The bar closed at about 10.00 p.m. and I made my way home to 79 Wood Street, about 100 yards away. As I opened the front door, I heard a swishing sound followed by a tremendous explosion. I realized afterwards that the swishing sound was made by the parachute that was carrying the mine. The force of the explosion threw me past the front door, down the length of the passage and into the kitchen. I was covered with bricks, plaster and wood. Apart from a few small cuts, I was OK. My mother and sister who were both sheltering under the kitchen table were unhurt. The back of our house was completely demolished.

My father, who was serving with the police in Barnet, arrived home and we took my mother and sister to his brother's house in Carnarvon Road for the night.

I myself went back to Oakmere, which was completely flattened, and helped the ARP and rescue people to dig out the bodies that were buried under the rubble. Some of those who had been killed that night were the nurses I had spent the evening with.

Tom's parents moved into a police house in Hillside Gardens, and later moved back to 79 Wood Street, after it had been rebuilt.

On one night alone, Sunday 22 September 1940, six German parachute mines were dropped on the Golders Green district. Another fell on Colindale Tube

Willifield Green in Hampstead Garden Suburb, one of the most attractive parts of the borough, and many surrounding houses in Coleridge Walk were completely destroyed by bombing. King George and Queen Elizabeth visited the site to show their solidarity with and support for local residents.

station just as a train was pulling out. According to the *Hendon Times*, hardly a shop front in Golders Green Road survived, and the road surface resembled 'a snow of glass'.

INCENDIARY BOMBS

Incendiary bombs were made mostly from phosphorous and magnesium which burn fiercely. They would penetrate roof tiles and start small fires in the rafters, which were often very difficult to get at. The intention was to swamp the fire service with many simultaneous demands. In the London Docks in 1941 incendiary bombs combined to form huge conflagrations which the fire services were powerless to control.

German Junkers JU 88 bombers carried incendiary bombs weighing a kilo (roughly 2 lb) in a kind of container sometimes nicknamed a 'Molotov basket'.

One such device was dropped over Finchley on the night of 19 February 1944. This was the effect it had on the houses of Ravensdale Avenue, North Finchley:

House Number		
	23	bomb in garage
	29	bomb in garage; another bomb in footpath and gate opposite
	41	bomb through roof
	43	ditto
	45	ditto
	47	ditto
	49	two bombs in road outside
	26	one bomb in back garden
	32	one bomb unexploded in road
	34	one bomb in front garden
	36	one bomb on garage roof, one in front garden and one in back garden
	38	one bomb fell through roof to ground floor, three in front garden
	40	three bombs in house, three unexploded in front garden, eight unexploded in road
	42	one bomb in front garden

A report in the *Finchley Press*, January 1941, describes how women and children helped to smother incendiary bombs that were dropped by a daylight raider:

One schoolboy is proud of the fact that he helped to put out three in one garden, while in a street nearby the milkman put out seven. In other cases housewives fended for themselves.

A number fell in a school playground while the children were having lessons, and a window was broken, but the bombs were soon put out by teachers.

Miss Reynolds was alone in the house with her 77-year-old mother, who is an invalid. A shower of incendiaries fell around her house. Her neighbour, Mrs

Hare, extinguished one by emptying a bucket of sand on it. Miss Reynolds was getting her mother to the reinforced room. Another neighbour, Mrs Morgan-Webb, then came and said 'Do you know that there is an incendiary on your roof?' The bomb had burned through the slates onto the rafters and was burning through the ceiling. The Fire Brigade was called and they managed to climb along the rafters and put out the bomb, which was filling the top landing with smoke. Miss Reynolds spoke of the wonderful way neighbours helped each other.

Two incendiary bombs fell adjacent to the house of Mr C.C. Morgan-Webb. One burned itself out on the lawn and his wife dealt with the other.

Mrs Parrott had a lucky escape when a bomb burst through her roof, but landed in the water tank. A neighbour came in with a stirrup pump, but the bomb was already spent.

Special Constable Jack Prime remembers how difficult it could be to deal with incendiaries:

I was in bed one day after being on night shift when a load of incendiaries fell in the Oakleigh Road area. One fell in a house in Loring Road where it landed on a bed which it set alight. When I got to the scene, the occupants had thrown buckets of garden soil onto the bed but it still continued to burn. We decided to throw the burning mattress out of the window but by that time there was so much earth on it that it took four people to do the job.

THE V1

In 1944 and 1945 Germany launched its two so-called 'V' weapons against the British Isles. They were designed as a revenge for the destruction of Germany by the Allied airforces.

The first of these, the V1, popularly known as the doodlebug or buzz-bomb, was a pilotless flying bomb powered by a simple jet engine and housing 1 ton of explosive. It was the distinctive noise of its engine which sounded like a large clumsy insect in flight that gave rise to its name. When the weapon ran out of fuel and the engine stopped there was a terrifying 10 second silence before it hit the ground. The weapon gave rise to particular anger since it was untargeted.

Three local residents of the time remember their experiences of V1 attacks:

'Look out! It's coming down!' I heard my father shout. The next moment there was a bright flash of light through the window, and then the house crashed down around us. I curled myself into a small ball as the bricks and mortar tumbled down, burying us in a sort of cave. The stairway still stood, making a roof. The bricks stopped falling and there was silence except for my father's faint voice calling. He had ducked under the sink. I sat as still as I could and listened to my sister reciting the Lord's Prayer. I kept thinking about my chocolate cake and wishing that I had eaten it. Gradually the sound of digging came nearer until I could hear my father's voice telling me to sit still. At last

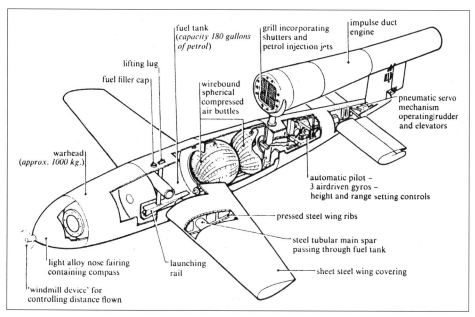

How the flying bomb worked. The above drawing is based on one issued by the government, and widely reproduced in the press.

there was a light in the hole near my head. Slowly it grew bigger until I could see my father's grimy face through it. A few minutes more shovelling and my father was lifting me out into the sunlight. All that was left was a heap of rubble, except for the chimney which was still standing.

The noise woke me just before the explosion when a great flame burnt my eyeballs. There was dead silence from cut-out to explosion. The thing had caught on the telegraph pole opposite and brought it down, and the whole lot had landed in my neighbour's garden. The gas main caught light which caused a big fire. The upstairs of the house fell on us bit by bit, also part of the outside wall. The wall seemed to float down like a feather, and yet we had an awful job to get it off the pillows. I started to struggle, but my husband pulled me under the blankets with him, drew it over our heads, held my hand tight and said, 'Wait till it stops dropping on us.' So we did, and by this time the children were sitting up and crying. The front door had gone and we were open to the street and the noise and the fire, which frightened them. So we all moved under the stairs and waited for help to come.

What a nightmare! I reached the top of the road and there were barriers up. There were ambulances, fire engines and police cars, and people were digging like mad trying to get people out. We lived in an upstairs flat and my daughter was in bed at the time. Her bed fell down two floors. She was trapped with a beam across her neck and another across her ankles. They had to cut through

EAST BARNET URBAN DISTRICT COUNCIL

EVACUATION

Evacuation Is now available for the following classes of persons :—

A.—School Children
   (unaccompanied)

B.—Mothers with Children of School age or under

C.—Expectant Mothers

who have been made homeless by enemy action since 12th June, 1944, and have not been rehoused.

1.—Application should be made for a Certificate of Homelessness to the Rehousing Department, No. I, Lyonsdown Road, New Barnet.

2.—When the Certificate has been received it should be presented at the Registration Centre at the Town Hall, Station Road, New Barnet.

From June 1944 people made homeless by Hitler's so-called secret weapons, the V1 and V2, and as yet not rehoused, were eligible for evacuation.

the wood before they could get her out. The puppy we had was in bed with her, and he saved her life because he made a noise like a baby crying and they knew where to look in the rubble.

Two wards at Colindale Hospital collapsed on 30 June 1944 when a V1 bomb fell in Edgware. Those killed were Percy Young, William Pearson, George Loft, Edwin Lawrence, Robert Latimer, Nurse M. Ross, Violet Lewing, Mrs D. Burgess, Marion Silver and Joan Sayers. Another V1 narrowly missed Mill Hill barracks on 20 August of the same year.

THE V2

In July 1944 a secret Home Office circular (No. 1175A) warned that the enemy had developed long range rockets, nicknamed the V2. These carried about a ton of explosive, and because they flew some 40 miles high and exceeded the speed of sound, there was no warning of their approach. All civil defence personnel were asked to be especially watchful.

On 20 January 1945 a V2 rocket exploded in Calton Road, East Barnet, causing great destruction and loss of life. This official account, written shortly afterwards, shows the extent of the damage and how many people cooperated in the rescue and repair effort:

On the day following the incident, 423 building trades men, 30 military and over 300 civil defence workers were engaged on immediate house repairs. About a third of this force started work the same afternoon. Snow and sharp frost which lasted many days hampered work.

The temporary covering of windows was substantially complete by the day following. Altogether 11,000 yards super of felt, 1,200 yards of translucent material, 100,000 feet of laths and 25 cwt of nails were used in this work.

By 15 Feb, over 150,000 roof tiles had been relaid. 60 cold water storage tanks, 60 lavatory basins and 1,250 WC pans have been supplied. 25,000 square feet of glass has been fitted and a further 8,000 is on order. Over four tons of putty has been used.

It has been estimated that over 2 acres of ceiling board has been used. There is great difficulty in getting doors.

130 men were employed on salvaging furniture.

Approximately 60 yards of foul water and surface sewers have been destroyed.

Casualty Service
(a) Doctors: Six doctors were available at the site, later two were sent to Church Farm First Aid Post.
(b) First Aid: Three doctors were in attendance with 8 nurses. 48 casualties were seen.
(c) Heavy Unit: This was set up at 5 Netherlands Road. Two doctors, a sister and 7 nurses dealt with 30 cases.
(d) Light Unit: A doctor, a nurse and auxiliary nurses dealt with 22 minor cases.
(e) Ambulances: the four East Barnet Ambulances were assisted by four others from Wood Green and Tottenham.
(f) Hospitals:

Wellhouse	took	49
Friern		11
Victoria		1
Oakdene medical rest centre		12

Rescue
Two heavy rescue and one light rescue teams from East Barnet were helped by 11 heavy rescue teams from other districts. Reliefs for those parties were supplied by a further 18 rescue parties. Military, Home Guard and Police also helped.

Specially trained dogs were used to locate buried casualties and two bodies were recovered in this way.

Wardens
The first report was received at Control within 2 minutes and was sent by a 73 year old warden from a seriously damaged house in Dalmeny Road. Over 300 wardens from the district helped house holders with minor problems.

Rest Centre
St Mary's Hall in Church Hill Road was used for meals and many people had a quick wash and brush up. 21 people stayed overnight and a further 8 stayed elsewhere.

The rest centre was closed after four days.

Mortuary
As in all previous instances, the mortuary service was very efficient.

Women's Voluntary Services
Members of the WVS manned and operated the Incident Inquiry Point, the Mobile Emergency Feeding Unit and the Mobile Canteens at the incident.

Since that time, they have visited and helped casualties in hospital, helped rehouse families, provided furniture and curtains.

The Mobile Canteen is still at the site serving the reconstruction workers.

Military and Police
Military vehicles were used to move furniture away and to fetch building materials. A Police loudspeaker van was used. The Police took personal details of all casualties and others involved.

The street lights were turned on to help with night demolition work. Special deliveries of coal were made to damaged houses.

Allan Rolfe, a member of the East Barnet Civil Defence who lived in nearby Netherlands Road, was about to tuck into lunch on that winter morning when the icy calm was suddenly disrupted. Allan remembers the front door of his house hurtling down the hallway, narrowly missing his wife. They did not hear the vicious V2 rocket land, just the sounds of the houses in Calton Road being reduced to matchsticks, their roofs being torn off and the windows of their own front room shattering. It was twenty minutes before the shock of the explosion wore off. Allan recalls what happened next:

We were in such a state we didn't know what to do. Eventually I brought myself to have a look. You couldn't go outside – the air was thick with dust and muck. The bomb had dropped in the middle of Calton Road and the houses around were reduced to rubble.

The awful thing was knowing the people who were buried. In those days there was a household register. I used to keep a tally of everybody in Calton Road, so I had to identify the bodies.

We were digging people out. There was absolute chaos. One man was buried up to his neck. Another, a friend of mine, was killed. Every Saturday he used to bring home a bottle of beer. That Saturday, he was killed outright – but that bottle of beer was still standing.

It was the most devastating bombing we ever experienced. There were fourteen killed and countless injured. It took months to clean up, but then new houses were up, our own house was repaired and that was that.

There's not a thing to show what happened. It's mostly new people in the street now, and I'm sure a lot of them don't even realize the terrible catastrophe that took place.

Other V2s landed in the area. One hit the Prince Albert pub in Golders Green on a Sunday morning in January 1945. Fortunately the pub was closed and there

A V2 being prepared for launching.

were only a few casualties. Another fell at New Southgate opposite the gas works near the North Circular Road.

The 1,115th and last V2 rocket to hit the UK fell on 27 March 1945 at Kynaston Road, Orpington. The total casualties from rockets were 2,855 killed and 6,268 seriously injured. Those from flying bombs were 6,139 and 17,239 respectively. Compared both with the casualties inflicted on the Germans by British and American, and with the boastful forecasts made by Hitler, these figures are very small.

THE POWER OF TEA AND PRAYER

The following two accounts give a vivid impression of what life was like during the bombing and the rocket attacks. The first story comes from the *Hendon Times* of February 1941:

SCHOOLBOY WAS RAID HERO

Twelve year old Keith Gurnett, whose home is in the middle of a row of cottages, was sleeping in a downstairs room with his brother and sister, when a bomb fell on the block. Mrs Gurnett said, 'My husband and I were sleeping in the next room. There was a rushing sound and a huge explosion. If it had not been for Keith throwing himself over the baby, she would have been killed by a piece of ceiling which fell onto her cot. It was a miracle that the seven of us escaped. We were all suffering from shock, but you can soon shake that off with willpower and a cup of tea.'

The second account is in the form of a series of extracts from the diary kept by two auxiliary nuns of the Convent of the Good Shepherd, in Finchley. Their words give us an interesting insight into her attitude to the German raids. The diary begins in 1940.

20 Aug 1940: Today being the Feast of the Assumption, Mother let the children go into the field to play about 10.00 a.m. Shortly afterwards a most queer mournful sound came, it seemed, out of the sky. It was the siren and it meant German aircraft overhead. All made for the refuge room, and all at once we looked for Mother. She had gone off into a quiet corner to pray and was unconscious of what had happened. The raid lasted about half an hour.

24 Aug: The second raid commenced at 10 to 4 in the afternoon. Mother made us put on our gas masks for practice and to pass the time. We also had a fire drill which was very funny, the water went all over the floor instead of on the imaginary bomb.

26 Aug: The raid started just as we were having afternoon tea. However we were not to be outdone by Hitler, and tea was served in the air raid shelter. We had tea in our bowls and bread and butter in our hands and it was lovely. We thoroughly enjoyed it.

12 Sep: My night for fire watching. At about 10.45 p.m. we heard 2 very big shots from a cannon and it made me shoot out of bed. I got lost looking for Mildred in the dark in the cloisters and she for me and we had no torch. I got nervous wondering what would happen if Mother came and found us wandering round the cloister instead of at our post on the landing. Anyway we managed to get back to the dormitory and Maria came with a torch.

14 June 1943: We were spending the afternoon in the field as it was Whit Monday and at about 3 p.m. a plane passed over and lost control and came down in St Pancras Cemetery. It appears that the wing came off the plane. We thought we were done for as the place where the plane crashed is about one minute by air from us. Another wonderful sign of God's care for us.

7 Oct: Tonight I saw a Gerry caught in the searchlights and a lot of incendiary bombs were dropped on Highgate and Finchley. The guns were very fierce for some time.

26 June 1944: One bold doodle came right over our shelter. It seemed to come down within a few yards of us. We heard the whine of its propeller and really thought it was the end for us. Mother gave us the Absolution and we all laid and waited for the end. But God was looking after us again, but some poor souls are sent to eternity.

8 May 1945: Today is Victory day and the Germans have surrendered. The nation is keeping today and tomorrow as holidays to celebrate the great occasion. Thank God for delivering us from our enemies. The sky is ablaze with fireworks and bonfires.

FOUR

On the Home Front

The term 'home front' was an imaginative one. It recognized that the way people organized themselves in their own home was as important to the war effort as the actions of the armed forces. To help them, propaganda and information campaigns appeared everywhere: in the local newspapers such as the *Barnet Press*, on poster hoardings in every high street and in daily radio broadcasts.

FOOD AND RATIONING

The feeding of Britain and the maintenance of the nation's health over a period of more than six years is one of the more remarkable stories of the war.

Before the conflict, 60 per cent of our food and raw materials came from abroad, much of it from the Commonwealth. It was obvious to all that such supplies would be threatened by Germany's U-boat fleet so plans were laid well in advance for the rationing of food and other scarce materials.

Finchley's town clerk, R.M. Franklin, was in charge of food control. He recalls how ration books were printed and other preparations made, well before September 1939:

> In April 1939 I received a coded message from the Ministry of Food instructing us to start the issue of ration cards. One of the borough's librarians, Seymour Smith, took over the enormously detailed work involved, and he had an office and small staff over the Gas showrooms in Regents Park Road. A national advertising campaign told people what they must do and it all went smoothly in spite of the complexity.

This was another example of the wisdom of appointing local people with the right kind of experience to carry out detailed tasks.

Rationing of food started in January 1940, and was widely seen as fair and reasonable. Up to that time, much irritation had been caused by wealthier sections of the community buying large quantities of goods that were likely to be in short supply, forcing up prices and causing local shortages. Now food coupons covering the staple foods were issued to everyone and prices were controlled. Citizens had to register with the grocer, butcher and milkman of their choice for their weekly allowances. Each district had a food supply committee to organize the distribution of foods to the shops.

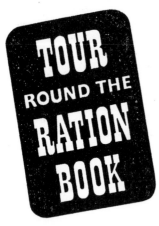

This year's Ration Book is a much simpler affair than last year's three books, and you should get familiar with it from the start. So here we take you on a conducted tour, with stops at the principal objects of interest! Cut this out and read it with the Ration Book in front of you. Then you will see how simple it has all been made.

THE CHILD'S BOOK
R.B.2. will be used in exactly the same way except that the tea coupons will be marked when oranges are bought, and will not be cut out.

YOUR OLD RATION BOOKS should be kept until the end of August. They may still be needed – for instance for July preserves, or your first tin of dried eggs. If they contain special authorisations keep them until these are used up. Do not transfer them to your new book.

THE FRONT COVER. Check the entries with your identity card. If there is any difference report it to the Food Office.

PAGE 2 You should by now have filled in the details at X. See that they agree with those on the front cover. Fill in Y if under 18. Leave Z alone.

PAGE 5 is the first of the coupon pages. See how they are now all divided (Points as well) into four-weekly periods numbered 1 to 13. This will help you to "keep your place" and make shopping easier. You have re-registered by now of course, so the counterfoils have been cut out by the shops. You need not fill in the spaces marked B unless you deposit whole pages with your retailer.

PAGE 9 now combines in one the coupons for butter, margarine and cooking fats.

PAGE 11 will be used for the ordinary and the special ration of cheese.

PAGE 13 will record your purchase of eggs. Remember that you won't get them every week. Poultry keepers will get no shell eggs.

PAGE 15 combines sugar and preserves. The squares marked Q, R, S will not be used at present.

PAGE 17 Tea coupons will be cut out by the retailer, four at a time.

PAGES 25 TO 34 are Points Coupon pages. They are just the same as those in the old pink book but the four-week periods are referred to by number instead of date.

PAGE 25 MUST CONTAIN THE NAMES AND ADDRESSES OF YOUR RETAILERS. It is illegal to use the Ration Book if these are not filled in. The column on the left is for noting the deposit of whole pages.

PAGE 39 Fill in if you deposit any rows of Points Coupons, also fill in the bottom line if you deposit your tea coupon page. Note this specially because it is new.

BACK COVER (page 40) has two panels. Panel 1 (at the top) will be used for soap, which may still be bought at any time during the four-weekly period. Panel 2 will not be used yet.

Advertisements were used to explain the workings of the ration book.

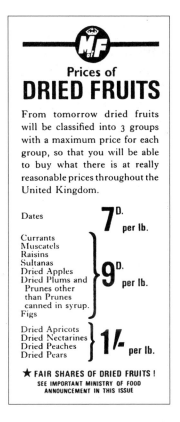

'Fair shares for all' was a popular slogan but not always a fact of life.

In those early months, when only essential foods were rationed, money could still buy a variety of non-rationed items, such as tinned goods. At the end of 1941, however, the so-called 'points' scheme was introduced, whereby each person was allowed sixteen points per month to be spent as he or she wished on goods such as breakfast cereals, tinned foods, rice and preserves.

Although the amount of rations varied accordingly to availability and seasons of the year, the following is a typical allowance per person:

Item	Weekly allowance
Bacon or ham	4–8 oz
Cheese	1–8 oz
Butter	1–8 oz
Eggs	½–4
Milk	½–2 pints
Tea	2–4 oz
Sugar	8–16 oz
Sweets and chocolate	2–4 oz
National Dried Milk	1 tin (= 4 pints) every 4 weeks
Dried eggs	1 packet (= 12 eggs) every 8 weeks

For most people, one of the hardest crosses to bear was the miniscule tea ration – the British 'cuppa' was sacrosant and any attempt to reduce it still further would have played havoc with morale. Meat was also rationed, initially at 1s 10d (9p) worth per week, later reduced to 1s 2d (6p) of which 'two penn'orth must be taken in corned beef'. Products such as sausages and fish were not rationed but disappeared 'under the counter', as did many other things such as cigarettes and spirits. From time to time, allocations of unrationed products in short supply were distributed by local shop keepers and were sold largely 'to registered customers only' – a rich source of vulgar humour and music hall jokes. Beer was officially watered down.

Confectionery, which had virtually disappeared from the shops, was rationed to 2 oz per person per week in 1942 – a particular hardship for the traditional British 'sweet tooth'. In that same year, the white loaf disappeared to be replaced by the 'national wholemeal loaf' – a dull grey, tasteless but more nutritious commodity. Neither bread nor potatoes were rationed in the war years, and there were generally adequate supplies of fresh vegetables (see next section).

Hendon had a local committee which reported back to the Ministry of Information once a month. Its members consulted men and woman in the area about matters which concerned or interested them. The report for 1 September 1943 observes:

There is, however, one item which arouses more bad temper and that is the shortage of fish. Jews particularly are affected because they cannot eat several articles such as home-killed meat unless it has been passed by a Jewish butcher. They rely greatly on fish and a shortage of this hits them hard. Many complaints about fish are heard from all classes.

Another section of the report amplifies the problem:

There is undoubtedly a special grievance about fish supplies. This condition may be peculiar to Hampstead, Golders Green and Hendon. It is common to see a queue before 9 a.m. at the fishmongers. The grievance is that people with few domestic responsibilities are able to leave their homes and get an advantage over the women who have chidren to get to school and other duties. An added irritation is that the queues are often substantially composed of foreigners.

The system of rationing recognized special needs: heavy manual workers such as miners and farm workers, for example, were entitled to extra cheese. Two new welfare schemes were introduced early in the war which vastly improved the health of the nation. The National Milk Scheme (1940) allocated to pregnant women, nursing mothers and young children one pint of milk per day; five- to six-year-old children got half a pint daily, and children at school were supplied with a third of a pint during the break if they wanted it. These were supplied at subsidized prices, and were free to those on low incomes. A Vitamin Welfare Scheme (1941) provided cheap or free concentrated orange juice and cod liver oil to pregnant women and young children.

How to make lemon curd using marrows in place of eggs. The advertisement ignored the fact that lemons were virtually unobtainable!

WOOLTON PIE

ooking time: about 1 hour   *Quantity:* 4 helpings

his pie is named after the Minister of Food—Lord Woolton. It
an adaptable recipe that you can change according to the
gredients you have available.

ice and cook about 1 lb of each of the following in salted water:
tatoes (you could use parsnips if topping the pie with mashed
tatoes), cauliflower, swedes, carrots—you could add turnips
o. Strain but keep ¾ pint of the vegetable water.
Arrange the vegetables in a large pie dish or casserole. Add a
tle vegetable extract and about 1 oz rolled oats or oatmeal to the
getable liquid. Cook until thickened and pour over the
getables; add 3–4 chopped spring onions.
Top with Potato Pastry or with mashed potatoes and a very
tle grated cheese and heat in the centre of a moderately hot oven
til golden brown. Serve with brown gravy.
This is at its best with tender young vegetables.

The
KITCHEN FRONT

122 WARTIME RECIPES

broadcast by Frederick Grisewood,
Mabel Constanduros and others, specially selected by the Ministry of Food.

*A selection of wartime recipes and advertisements including the legendary Woolton Pie, named
after the then Minister of Food.*

Above: Civic or British Restaurants were organized by local councils and were intended to help supplement the official rations. Finchley's first Civic Restaurant was at the Hamilton Hall in Ballards Lane, Finchley. Lady Woolton (wife of the Minister for Food) and Alderman Wilmot, the Mayor of Finchley, acted as unpaid servers at the opening ceremony.
Left: A typical menu from a British Restaurant. Money was paid to the cashier as you entered the building. This was exchanged for coloured plastics discs – different colours for different courses.

Huge sums of money were spent by the Ministry of Food on advertising and promotion in order to inform people of ways of keeping the family fit and saving food. Recipes were designed to make the best of a limited and dull – but nutritious – range of foodstuffs. Top artist and copywriters produced memorable campaigns with cartoon figures such as Potato Pete and Dr Carrot explaining the benefits and delights of those two important vegetables. A particularly popular figure was Charles Hill, the Radio Doctor renowned for his plain speaking, who appeared in a five-minute daily Kitchen Front programme which followed immediately after the 8 a.m. news bulletin. One result of such campaigns was a 60 per cent increase in the consumption of potatoes. A campaign to use a national glut of carrots maintained that carrots increased night-time visibility and hinted that, by eating lots of them the ordinary citizen could achieve the keen eyesight of the legendary fighter pilot 'Cats-Eye' Cunningham. It was all in a good cause.

The wasting of food was a crime punishable by substantial fines. At Barnet magistrates court in 1941, for example, a Miss M.B. was fined a total of £10 with 2 guineas costs, and her servant 5s (25p), for wasting bread by feeding it to the birds.

Clubs were formed to keep poultry, rabbits, pigs and bees. There was even a regular column in the *Finchley Press* specifically for their interest. Woodhouse School, Finchley, for example, ran a poultry club (six dozen chickens in an old guinea-pig run) as well as a fruit and vegetable garden. Such activities, it was felt, were valuable training in animal husbandry as well as a source of income and contribution to the war effort. Strict limits were placed on the number of animals that could be kept: more than twenty hens, for example, meant that some eggs had to be handed over to the Ministry.

The ability to 'eat out' if you had both time and money was legitimate but felt by many to be unfair. It was curtailed in 1942 by a series of legal restrictions which limited the individual to paying 5s for a meal (25p) and ensured the closure of restaurants by 11 p.m. or midnight in certain areas.

Much more important for the war effort was the institution of communal feeding centres called British Restaurants in areas subjected to air raids. They served nutritious, well-balanced meals at a reasonable price and proved very popular. They were often located in church and community halls and staffed by the WVS.

As months went by, more and more goods became scarce and disappeared 'under the counter': torch batteries, shoelaces, matches, cigarettes, whisky, cooking utensils and, the source of much humour, knicker elastic. Many people resorted to the black market for such goods, as it was necessary to queue for hours to get goods in short supply.

The first commodity to be rationed was petrol, which depended entirely upon oil imports and was a particular hazard for the merchant ships that had to carry it. There was considerable criticism that supplies for private motoring (6 gallons a month) were still available as late as March 1942. Matters came to a head when cinema newsreels showed pictures of burning oil-tankers and the crowds at the 1941 Epsom Derby with its busy car park.

In June 1941 clothes and textiles became rationed. Initially each person was allocated sixty-six coupons a year to spend on what they wished. This was soon

"DRIED EGGS are my eggs — my whole eggs and nothing but my eggs"

Dried eggs are the complete hen's eggs, both the white and the yolk, dried to a powder. Nothing is added. Nothing but moisture and the shell taken away, leaving the eggs themselves as wholesome, as digestible and as full of nourishment and health-protecting value as if you had just taken the eggs new laid from the nest. So put the eggs back into your breakfast menus. And what about a big, creamy omelette for supper? You can have it savoury; or sweet, now that you get extra jam.

DRIED EGGS build you up!

In war-time, the most difficult foods for us to get are the body-builders. Dried eggs build muscle and repair tissue in just the same way as do chops and steaks; and are better for health-protection. So we are particularly lucky to be able to get dried eggs to make up for any shortage of other body-builders such as meat, fish, cheese, milk.

Your allowance of DRIED EGG is equal to 3 eggs a week

You can now get one 12-egg packet (price 1/3) per 4-week rationing period — three fine fresh eggs a week, at the astonishingly low price of 1¼d. each. Children (holders of green ration books) get two packets each rationing period. You buy your dried eggs at the shop where you are registered for shell eggs; poultry keepers can buy anywhere.

Don't hoard your dried eggs; use them up — there are plenty more coming!

Note.   *Don't make up dried eggs until you are ready to use them; they should not be allowed to stand after they've been mixed with water or other liquid. Use dry when making cakes and so on, and add a little more moisture when mixing.*

FREE — DRIED EGG LEAFLET containing many interesting recipes, will be sent on receipt of a postcard addressed to Dept. 627E, Food Advice Service, Ministry of Food, London, W.1.

ISSUED BY THE MINISTRY OF FOOD   (S.74)

Dried eggs came from the USA under the Lease-Lend scheme. They were convenient and nutritious but regarded by most people as a poor second to fresh eggs.

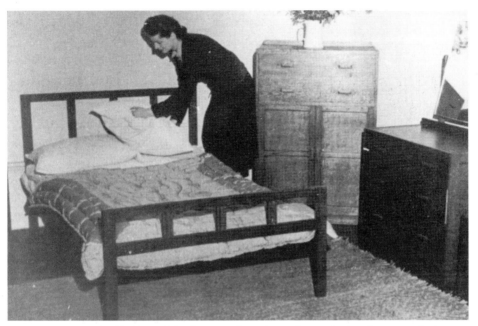

There was a considerable demand for furniture from those who required replacements for items destroyed by enemy action, as well as from newly married couples. The Utility scheme used top designers to create a limited range of furniture which was simple, inexpensive and of specified quality. It was very popular and, of course, rationed.

reduced to forty-four coupons. The government also introduced 'utility clothes'. These were garments designed by some top fashion designers which were based on a limited range of fabrics, simple in design and much cheaper than more conventional clothes. They proved immensely popular, as did the kindred scheme for utility furniture designed to meet the shortages caused by air raids.

DIG FOR VICTORY

Much of the food obtained outside rationing came from people's own efforts to 'grow their own'. The campaign, called Dig for Victory, was among the most successful of the war. The amount of land under cultivation nationally was under 12 million acres in 1939. By 1945, however, around 18 million acres was being used and Britain was growing approximately two-thirds of its food requirements as opposed to one-third in 1939.

The comparatively rural nature of our area made it easier for people to join the Dig for Victory campaign. In addition to extending existing allotments, green spaces such as parks, golf courses, playing fields, railway embankments and even roadside verges, cemeteries and bombed sites were turned over to growing vegetables such as potatoes, carrots, marrows and onions. Much harder for the

Friern Barnet's
DIG FOR VICTORY WEEK
July 5th to 10th in Friary Park

A WEEK OF MANY EVENTS—BUT MAKE A SPECIAL NOTE
OF THESE.

GRAND
CONCERT
and OPENING
CEREMONY

At British Restaurant, Saturday July 3rd.
Tickets 3/6 and 2/6 from 32, Glenthorne
Road, N.11.   Enterprise 3120.
Opening Ceremony by CMDR. CAMPBELL
B.B.C. Brains Trust.

PRODUCE
SHOW

On Friday & Saturday, July 9th & 10th in
Friary Park
Opening by CYRIL FLETCHER and
BETTY ASTELL
Prize Giving by MABEL CONSTANDUROS
Have you sent your entry form in yet ?

BRAINS
TRUST

On Saturday, July 10th at 3 p.m. Friary Park
Question Master FREDDIE GRISEWOOD, B.B.C.

OPENING OF THE EXHIBITION ON MONDAY JULY 5th at 2.30 p.m.
by RICHARD GOOLDEN ("Mr. Penny")

TALKS BY PERCY IZZARD (Daily Mail) and other experts.

Poultry and Rabbit Show ; Film Shows ; Private Gardens
Competition ; Pigs and Bees Exhibition ; Lectures ; Talks and
Demonstrations ; Cookery Competition ; Horticultural Exhibi-
tions ; Poultry Houses ; Garden Frames ; Children's Posters ;
Competitions for everyone.

200 Cash Prizes and Several Cups to be won.

The Dig for Victory campaign had its lighter moments.

Do you remember when the headlines said—

"No potatoes for this Sunday's joint"

While thousands of housewives enjoyed another
little grumble, the wiser families who had dug for
victory enjoyed their Sunday joint with all the
potatoes and other vegetables they wanted.   Learn
from experience.   To be sure of the family's vegetables, you must grow them yourselves—women and
older children as well as men.   If you haven't a garden,
ask your Local Council for an allotment.   Start to

DIG FOR VICTORY NOW!

POST THIS COUPON NOW *(Unsealed envelope, 1d. stamp)*

TO MINISTRY OF AGRICULTURE, HOTEL LINDUM, ST. ANNES-ON-SEA, LANCS.
Please send me copies of free pictorial leaflets, "How to Dig" and "How to Crop"

NAME ....

ADDRESS ....
                                                        B.99

ISSUED   BY   THE   MINISTRY   OF   AGRICULTURE

citizen was to replace his or her treasured garden lawns and flower beds with vegetable plots – but the sacrifice was made as part of the war effort. Even window boxes were used to grow crops such as lettuce and tomatoes.

Leaflets and advertisements by the hundreds bombarded people on the what, where and how to grow their own vegetables and keep livestock. Garden clubs were formed which, drawing upon the considerable experience of allotmenteers, supplied on a collective basis items such as tools, seeds, national fertilizer and, most important, advice from the more experienced gardeners.

THE WOMEN'S LAND ARMY

The vital importance of food in wartime was recognized by the formation of the Women's Land Army (WLA) – an organization that had already proved its worth in the First World War.

British agriculture was still very much dependent on manual labour. The gaps

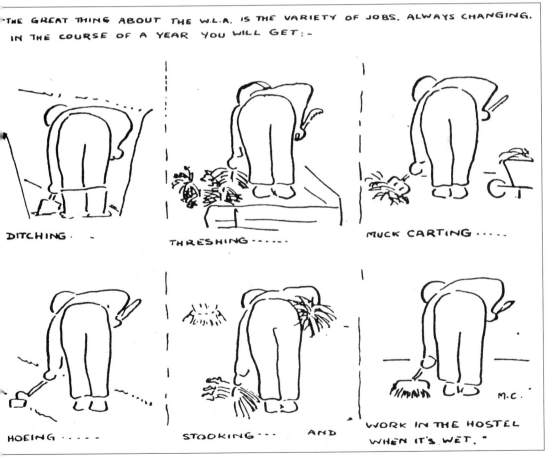

A light-hearted reminder of the WLA's many duties as featured in one of its magazines.

in the ranks of farm labourers drafted into the forces, and the growth in agriculture generally, were more than made up by recruits from the Women's Land Army. The Land Army girls, as they were known, were initially volunteers but later on were conscripted as an alternative to drafting into the armed services. Those that thought it might be a softer option were soon disillusioned: it was hard, badly paid work.

The wage in the early years of the war was 22s (£1.10) per week, plus board and lodgings. By 1944 this had increased to 48s, with only seven days' leave per year. Many girls were billeted on the farms in which they worked. There were also girls who worked in gangs on activities such as ploughing and harvesting. They moved from area to area and were often billeted in hostels. Many found the physical demands of the job too heavy and the work uncongenial. Others, including women from the towns, grew to love the work and the outdoor life.

In their corduroy breeches, woollen socks and felt hats, the Land Army girls were a distinctive sight. They had a hostel in Totteridge Park. A monthly local magazine called *Land Girl* reported in February 1945 that 'seven of our girls have passed the tractor driving test and N.J. Darke won the County Cup for ploughing'.

The magazine also gave practical advice to the girls: 'There are not enough gum boots and your County Officer will decide who is to wear them. There is no need to worry if they are too large, just wear several pairs of socks inside. Do NOT wear them to walk to and from work. Keep them clean. Remember that milk and oil are very bad for rubber boots. When your socks are worn out, save the remnants and use them as gloves or to patch other socks.'

SPEND, SAVE AND SALVAGE

In the war years too much money was chasing too few goods. By strictly controlling prices of essential goods, however, inflation was largely kept in check.

Many thousands of people in our own locale, now fully employed, found themselves paying income tax for the first time. This was not popular at the best of times, particularly when, in 1944, the Pay as You Earn Scheme was introduced, which made evasion more difficult. From 1941 onwards everyone contributed through purchase tax. This initially had a top rate of 33⅓ per cent, although the amount varied with each item purchased: luxury goods were taxed at the highest rate.

The campaign to get the population saving their money instead of spending it was one of the most successful of the war years. People were encouraged to believe that their savings money could actually 'buy' a fighter plane or ship and this led to intense efforts by the councils' National Savings committees. Of particular interest were four special events devoted respectively to War Weapons Week, Warship Week, Wings for Victory Week and Salute the Soldier, when each area set itself an ambitious savings target.

Finchley, for example, set itself a target of £500,000 in the Wings for Victory Week (6–13 March 1943). This would, it was implied, purchase a hundred fighter aircraft. Apart from all the banks and post offices which normally sold National

Exchange of plaques between HMS Tartar *and* Finchley *at Avenue House, 1942. Each local district 'adopted' a warship. Barnet had HMS* Cromer *(its crest can be seen in Barnet Museum), East Barnet adopted HMS* Musketeer, *Fiern Barnet HMS* Fantome, *and Hendon HMS* Ursa.

HMS Musketeer, *officially adopted by East Barnet, was a 'Laforey' class destroyer, launched on 2 December 1941 and displacing 1,920 tons. She carried six 4.7 inch guns and had a top speed of about 36 knots. She was specially insulated for service in high latitudes.*

The SQUANDER BUG
WILL GET YOU IF YOU DON'T WATCH OUT!

When the Squander Bugs put their heads together there's trouble brewing! They're out to stop your money helping the war. They'll do all they can to prevent you having a little nest-egg when peace comes. Fortunately, more and more sensible people are de-feating them by buying Savings Certificates regularly every week. Are *you* one of them?

Savings Certificates costing 15/- are worth 20 6 in 10 years—increase free of income tax. They can be bought outright, or by instalments with 6d., 2/6 or 5/- Savings Stamps through your Savings Group or centre, or at any Post Office or Trustee Savings Bank. Buy now!

ISSUED BY THE NATIONAL SAVINGS COMMITTEE

Our men—they joke
on the eve of battle.
They go forward
never faltering,
never dismayed,
on the road to victory.
They shall lack nothing
our support
can give them.
We are in duty bound—
each one of us
—to SALUTE
THE FIGHTING FORCES
with more
and yet more saving!

"REPAIR SQUAD, PLEASE!"

Yesterday . . . in the garage . . . repairing cars . . . "a little trouble with the plugs, sir ? Soon get that fixed !" Today a soldier—Right in the thick of it . . . shells bursting . . . snipers taking a crack at him. But he does it ! And repairs another tank—ready for action ! Salute his toughness—his endurance !

Salute the Soldier — with more savings ! Let us all vow today to mobilize our money — by cutting spending and increasing lending. Let us lend to our country — and so lend practical help to "the boys out there !"

SALUTE THE SOLDIER

Issued by the National Savings Committee

The Squander Bug was one of the most imaginative cartoon characters of the war years. He was used as the basis of many campaigns to save rather than spend.

Savings stamps, twelve selling centres were set up in shops, wardens' posts and private houses staffed by the WVS, wardens and householders. An elaborate launch programme was arranged and competitions run for local schools to design posters and models with an appropriate theme. These were exhibited in the libraries at East and North Finchley.

A tribute was paid in the local newspaper to the boys of Clark's College who had arranged for a 500 lb bomb to be exhibited on which the public could stick stamps so that it might be filled and dropped over Germany. One ex-Finchley schoolboy used to withdraw all his savings before 'the big event' and reinvest it during the savings week.

Finchley exceeded its target handsomely, collecting no less than £623,462 in the seven days. Friern Barnet also exceeded its £150,000 target by £45,000.

Another key wartime task was the saving and salvaging of everything capable of being reworked or reused. We are still suffering from its effects fifty years later, as many fine iron railings and ornamental gates were removed from public and private buildings in January 1940. People were led to believe that these would be

> ### EAST BARNET URBAN DISTRICT COUNCIL.
>
> ### SALVAGE OF WASTE MATERIALS
>
> # DO NOT WASTE YOUR PAPER
>
> The Council will collect all your waste paper including newspaper, cardboard, magazines, old books, etc.
>
> Please keep your paper and place it on your dust bin or give it to the dustman when he calls each week.
>
> # RAW MATERIAL IS WAR MATERIAL

The public were encouraged to save almost anything as part of their contribution to the war effort.

turned into tanks and battleships but about three-quarters of such metal was unsuitable for use and it remained for years in the piles into which it had been placed by voluntary organizations such as the WVS, Scouts, Guides and Boys' Brigade. Places in Finchley to suffer in this way included Victoria Park, Avenue House and Woodhouse School.

By July 1940 the salvage drives embraced many materials. A special appeal was made by Lady Reading on 10 July for aluminium to build Spitfires. Neighbours vied with each other to donate pots, pans, fittings and even thimbles. Even family photograph frames and childrens' toys were donated to the cause. Here again, the metal was mostly unsuitable for use.

Apart from scrap metal and paper, separate piles were made for rubber, tins, bones, rags, bottles and jars. Kitchen scraps were placed in dustbins allocated to streets and collected by the WVS for turning into pig food called Tottenham Pudding. Here is a public appeal put out by Friern Barnet's WVS via a loud speaker mounted on a car touring the streets:

Hullo. Hullo. This is Friern Barnet WVS calling. During the next fortnight we are having a kitchen waste drive. Every scrap of kitchen waste is needed. Potato peelings, bread crusts, waste vegetable leaves and all kitchen waste scraps. Now this does not mean mouldy bread, tea leaves, coffee grounds or any waste which

Bins for the collection of household scraps to be used for pig food were a common sight on the streets.

has come into contact with soap or soda or other irritant. So keep it clean. And here is another very important matter. Take it to the bins provided for the purpose. These bins are provided by the council and emptied every day by WVS collectors. Every day mind you. So will you please see that they are filled up to capacity. Your kitchen waste goes to the feeding of pigs and it is vitally important that the tonnage of waste is maintained. If it is not, that means importing into the country which means ships and sailors' lives . . . make your contribution to raise the collection to 25 tons. Don't on any account burn it or put it on the compost heap. Just one last request. Ask your neighbour to do the same. It's the little lots that make all the difference.

A professional copywriter would be hard put to write a more effective message.

The shortages of just about everything making for a civilized existence led not only to long queues but efforts to repair things and economize. Here again, whimsical characters such as Mrs Sew & Sew and The Squander Bug were used in advertisements and on hoardings to give practical advice.

Superintendent Salvage, with Detector-Inspector Waste, take charge for the holidays

The Superintendent: *Now, Inspector, let's have your report.*

The Inspector: Well, sir, everything's mostly according to plan. I have my men in every house and a Sergeant acting directly under each grown-up Salvage Steward.

The Superintendent: *Good. How's the Bone Hunt progressing?*

The Inspector : Things are moving. My house constables check up on every joint that comes to the house and personally superintend plate clearance after each meal. They are also present at each emptying of the stock-pot and take account of all bones given to the dog. These are all reclaimed and put into the Bone Tin. Every other day, the house constable takes the tinful to the street collector's post and adds it to the bone collection.

The Superintendent: *What about fish bones?*

The Inspector: Ah, we don't make the mistake of putting *them* in, but all other little bones, even rabbit bones, are carefully salvaged.

The Superintendent: *Keep going—if every bone in every house is saved the country will have the bones to produce nitro-glycerine to propel hundreds of thousands of shells.*

The Inspector: The Waste-paper Search is going on relentlessly. The instructions are as follows : Every day, house constables collect the previous day's newspapers and any finished-with magazines, together with letters that have been answered and all wrappings from parcels.

The Superintendent: *String is included?*

The Inspector: Certainly—string is a vital ingredient in paper-making. Once a week old cheques and receipts are collected from the grown-ups and taken to the bank for repulping. No secrets leak out this way !

The Superintendent: *What about paid bills?*

The Inspector: They're collected once a week from Mothers' shopping baskets, and odd bus tickets are searched for, too, and the kitchen drawer inspected in case too many paper bags have accumulated.

The Superintendent: *Have you tracked down that case of Pig-swill Poisoning yet?*

The Inspector: Yes, sir ! At No. 4 Home Drive one constable was not alert enough in seeing that NO coffee grounds and rhubarb tops went into the bucket with vegetable trimmings and plate scrapings. He knows the seriousness of this slackness, and won't offend again.

The Superintendent: *Well, carry on, Inspector, and don't forget that the Case of the Elusive Rubber must be tackled next. Not an old hot-water bottle, a rubber boot, a worn-out rubber ring, or an old bicycle tyre must escape.*

The Inspector: Very good, sir. ·The Squad is on the job !

MOTHERS

Make the children responsible for Salvage Collections. They'll enjoy doing a worthwhile job and they'll probably help to keep you up to the mark yourself.

SALVAGE STEWARDS

The youngsters make good helpers—especially if you appeal to their imagination. The above are suggestions for getting them interested. Organise your Street Squad these holidays, and watch the Salvage pile up !

A reminder that everyone, even young children, could play their part in the war effort. Although amusing and relevant, today this appeal gives an uncomfortable impression of 'encouragement to sneak'.

Do you care for clothes?

IF YOU CARE FOR CLOTHES you naturally want to *take* care of your clothes. This is a really important war job for every woman to take seriously to-day. Fortunately you are rewarded for the extra trouble, not only by feeling that you are helping to win the war, but also by looking your best all the time. *And* you save money as well as coupons.

MAKE DO AND MEND

Every sailor knows his "rig" may have to last him a long time. So definite times are set aside each week for the sailors to " make and mend," clean and repair their clothes. Follow their example. Every time you avoid buying new clothes by mending, altering or " freshening up " something you already have you are definitely helping to beat Hitler and his gang.

PUT YOUR BEST FOOT FORWARD

There's a lot more wear to be got out of every pair of shoes than some people realise. Here are some simple hints. Never put your shoes near the fire or on a radiator. When leather is exposed directly to heat it soon dries up, curls out of shape and loses its toughness and flexibility. Never go out in new shoes for the first time in wet weather. Wear them indoors for a few days instead. Always rub polish well into leather shoes and brush suede and fabric shoes *before* you put them away—on shoe trees if you have them

A WRINKLE ABOUT WRINKLES

Creases and wrinkles should never be allowed to stay. When you take off your clothes at night shake them and smooth them and hang or fold them up at once. Crumples and wrinkles should be tackled at once, before they become " set," by using a damp cloth and a hot iron.

Count your Coupons

When you are thinking of buying some garment or piece of material, count over your coupons and think of the warm things that you will need in the winter time. The cold weather is only a few weeks ahead. Better hold your coupons. Perhaps you can " make do " for the present with the clothes you have. Once your coupons are gone they're gone.

ISSUED BY THE BOARD OF TRADE

ISSUED BY THE BOARD OF TRADE

NEW LIFE FOR OLD SHEETS

FIRST STEP — TEAR YOUR WORN SHEET DOWN THE CENTRE

Watch for signs of wear and deal with a sheet that needs it before there's a hole. Tear or cut it in half lengthwise and join the selvedges in a flat seam by hand. Then machine-hem the outer edges. These thin parts will go under the mattress where there's little strain on them, so your re-made sheet is almost as strong as when new.

NOT only sheets but *all* your household things must be made the very most of. These hints will help you to put off buying new.

USE SHEETS AND PILLOWCASES TURN AND TURN ABOUT, so that each gets its fair share of wear. Put newly laundered ones on top of the pile and take them out from underneath. Things not in constant use should not be stored in a hot cupboard as heat weakens the material. Save wear and tear by mending things that need it before they are washed, or at least by giving them " first-aid tacking." When the washing is done at home, avoid bleaching (which is an expert's job) or you may damage your things. Dry in the sun instead wherever possible. In ironing, take care the iron isn't too hot and never iron over the folds. Air everything thoroughly.

See to Stains at once. Practically all stains will come out if treated at once. Pour boiling water through tea and coffee stains while wet, then wash in the usual way—do the same with fruit stains. Don't forget that egg stains and blood stains should be soaked in *cold* water.

Things you can turn into Towels. A most serviceable bath towel can be made out of an old honeycomb bedspread that you are no longer using. Tea towels can often be made out of worn table runners, table mats, doyleys, etc., otherwise they should be put by for the duration to save laundering and mending. Never let things get too dirty before washing them : the extra rubbing is harmful and you use more soap in the end. Watch your towels for thin places and mend before holes come and before washing. When patches are needed. use old material—a new patch on a worn towel is apt to tear away. Two thin towels diamond-stitched together will make one strong one. Towels don't need to be ironed—rough drying will save time and wear.

● **JOIN A MAKE-DO & MEND CLASS**
Sewing and household jobbery classes and mending parties are being formed all over the country. Already there are hundreds of them in full swing. Any Citizens' Advice Bureau will be glad to tell you where and when your nearest class or party meets, and how you can join or help to form one in your own district.

Mend and Make-do
to save buying new

The advertisements on pp. 70–2 give a vivid impression of the government's efforts to encourage people to save and salvage.

ENTERTAINMENTS

One of the earliest casualties of the war, albeit briefly, was the 'entertainment business'. In September 1939 it was decreed that certain places where people gather in numbers should be closed to reduce casualties from bombing. Cinemas, theatres, concert and dance halls were among those affected, as were football and other sports grounds. The infant television service, based at Alexandra Palace, was also 'closed for the duration'.

For many people, the closure of the local cinema was the hardest to bear but, by the end of September, when it became apparent that the predicted mass slaughter would not take place, cinemas and theatres were allowed to open. By 1940, with the nation moving towards a total war effort, it was realized that recreation and entertainment was essential if people were to give of their best at work. The Rex cinema at East Finchley had a special showing for shiftworkers, and in February

EAST FINCHLEY'S CINEMA **REX** Telephone — TUDOR 2233 Manager — A. H. HUME

Today and Tomorrow — FOREIGN CORESPONDENT A   TILLEY OF BLOOMSBURY U

LATE FILMS FOR LATE WORKERS
Now Open for your entertainment—Weekdays till 10 p.m. Sundays 9 p.m.

SUNDAY JANUARY 19th
Open 3 p.m. to 9 p.m.

EDWARD G. ROBINSON CLARE TREVOR in

THE AMAZING DR. CLITTERHOUSE A
Screening at 4.39 & 7.37

◆

KAY FRANCIS in
COMET OVER BROADWAY A
Screening at 3.30 & 6.18

MONDAY, JANUARY 20th—   FOR THREE DAYS
MAUREEN O'HARA,   LOUIS HAYWARD in
DANCE, GIRL, DANCE A
Screening at 2.38, 5.38, 8.31 p.m.
ALSO
FAY WRAY,   CHARLES LANG in
WILD CAT BUS A
Screening at 1.15, 4.7, 7.7 p.m.
Last Complete Performance Commences at 7.7 p.m.

THURSDAY, JANUARY 23rd—   FOR THREE DAYS
RAY MILLAND,   LORETTA YOUNG in
THE DOCTOR TAKES A WIFE A
Screening at 2.45, 5.43, 8.41 p.m.
ALSO
OTTO KRUGER,   ONA MUNSON in
SCANDAL SHEET A
Screening pt 1.15, 4.13, 7.11 p.m.
Last Complete Performance Commences at 7.11 p.m.

Cinemas organized special film shows for shift workers and others unable to go to the pictures at the usual times as this advertisement from the winter of 1940/41 shows.

The members of the Civil Defence services organized many kinds of leisure activities, often to raise money for good causes. The Friern Barnet 'Arpettes' shown here were a popular act.

PROGRAMME

ARTISTES:

WALTER OLIVER	HARRY JEACOCKE
DOROTHY CLARE, L.R.A.M.	ANN SOUTTER
"ESOR"	KEN LEWIS
JESSIE JEACOCKE	RENE ASKEY
TED LLOYD	BERT GRICE
DIANA PHILBEY	JOAN CARTER
PERCY SOUTTER	JEREMY WHITE

AND

TED WIGMORE
("*Wiggy*")

WITH THE

"ARPETTES"

PEGGY FARRINGTON	EILEEN LANE
DORIS STONE	RAY MOULTON
DOROTHY FRIEND	DIANA PHILBEY
NANCY CARPENTER	GWYN STEELE

SUPPORTED BY THE

"ARPSICHORDS"

FRANK DUNCAN	GEORGE FAWCETT
HARRY JEACOCKE	BOB WILLIAMS
JACK TICKLE	GEOFFREY THORP
GEOFFREY SMITH	MAC. McCARTHY

AND

JOHNNY SCHOOLING

The producers desire to express their grateful thanks to the F.B.U.D.C. Emergency Committee for their sanction in regard to the use of this Hall, and to the Stretcher Party for any inconvenience caused by the occupation of the "Depot," also to the undermentioned for their assistance and co-operation.

Scenery built by - - - - -	TED CHAPMAN
Scenery painted by - - - -	DOROTHY CRUSE
Decorations designed by - - - -	KAY WILLS
Refreshments - - - - -	MRS. JAMES
Dances arranged by - - - -	PEGGY FARRINGTON
Grand Pianos kindly lent by	DR. BRANDER *(Friern Hospital)*
Orchestra under the direction of - - -	JOHN SCHOOLING
Lighting and Effects by - - - -	ALEC WILKINSON

The whole production under the joint supervision of

DORIS HAMMERSLEY AND JOHN GILPIN

1940 the General Officer Commanding the troops in London wrote asking the Odeon at Barnet to be opened on Sunday afternoons to give his soldiers 'something to do'.

Ballroom dancing, with its chance of meeting the opposite sex, was a particularly popular pastime. The Arcadia Dance Hall in Finchley Central gave free admission to Forces in uniform, and many local church halls and similar locations held Saturday night dances with profits going 'to a good cause'.

The war years disrupted the work of most professional symphony orchestras. In 1941 Sydney Beer formed the National Symphony Orchestra which gave regular concerts at the Ionic Cinema, Golders Green, featuring soloists such as Eileen Joyce, Moura Lympany and Solomon. The Carl Rosa Opera Company appeared there in 1944 with a roster of singers of the quality of Heddle Nash, Gwen Catley, Noel Eadie, Joan Hammond and Norman Allin.

This was above all, however, the era of the amateur concert party. To misquote Rutland Boughton: 'They laugh and are glad and are terrible.' A few were very good and some were of near professional standard, including some of the concert parties organized by people working in civil defence. As their work often involved long periods of inactivity, they used the time to write, produce and perform shows for local consumption. The Friern Barnet National Fire Service (NFS), for example, had a dance band, and one Air Training Corps (ATC) squadron ran a bugle and drum band.

Newsletters flourished. They were generally a mixture of light reading with sections on more serious subjects designed to improve work performance. The style of this poem from an April 1940 ARP newsletter is typical:

Form ARP/M1
Give Air Raid damage and your post
Then name the place that suffered most
What's caused the damage in the raid
How many are there needing aid.
Then Fire (that's always dealt with first)
What of the Mains, have any burst?
Has AR damage blocked a road?
Report a dud – it may explode.
Remember time and Service friends
Add your remarks and message ends.

It was to the radio (then called the wireless), however, that most people turned to for information and entertainment. It was perhaps, the most important instrument of communication with the population, and one that commanded respect. News broadcasts, often patriotic in tone, were avidly listened to – particularly when they were followed by one of Churchill's now legendary speeches. J.B. Priestley's broadcasts around the time of Dunkirk also brought comfort and hope to the population. They were classics.

There were two broadcasting channels: the Forces Programme and the Home Service. The former featured light entertainment; comedy shows such as ITMA and Band Wagon were particular favourites and among the first to coin comedy

WARDEN'S REPORT FORM. A.R.P./M.I.

Form of Report to Report Centres.

(Commence with the words) "AIR RAID DAMAGE"

Designation of REPORTING AGENT
(e.g., Warden's Sector Number)

POSITION of occurrence

TYPE of bombs :—H.E. Incendiary Poison Gas

Approx. No. of CASUALTIES :—
(If any trapped under wreckage, say so)

If FIRE say so :—

Damage to MAINS :—Water Coal Gas Overhead electric cables Sewers

Names of ROADS BLOCKED

Position of any UNEXPLODED BOMBS

Time of occurrence (approx.)

Services already ON THE SPOT or COMING :—

Remarks :—

(Finish with the words) "MESSAGE ENDS"

ORIGINAL } These words are for use with a report sent by messenger.
DUPLICATE } Delete whichever does not apply.

Form ARP/M1 was the key message document. It was also the basis of humour in the Finchley wardens' magazine.

catch-phrases. The Home Service covered more serious subjects such as symphony concerts and discussion and debate programmes such as the Brain's Trust.

Holidays of any kind were a rare luxury during the war years. The problems of travelling distances in overcrowded, infrequent trains, plus the lack of accommodation and poor food at the other end, were just a few of the hazards. An imaginative scheme was devised called 'Holidays at Home'. These were organized by the local councils, often staffed by the WVS, and designed to provide quality entertainment in local parks, schools and halls. Among other benefits, they kept schoolchildren occupied during the holidays when many parents were working.

Olive Dyke of the Friern Barnet WVS recalled:

> All sorts of events and entertainments were arranged in local parks. WVS provided the refreshments. Some of the famous people I remember who visited Friary Park at that time were Freddie Grisewood and Commander Campbell of the Brain's Trust, and the singers Ann Ziegler and Webster Booth who lived at Torrington Park and gave concerts in the church hall in Friern Barnet Lane. In Bethune Park, we carried a large tea urn around on one of those 'stop me and buy one' Walls Icecream tricycles.

FRIERN BARNET
HOLIDAYS AT HOME
FORTHCOMING ATTRACTIONS

Sunday, July 11th.

Classical Gramophone Concert. Friary Park. 3 p.m.
Metropolitan Concert Orchestra. Friary Park. 6.30 p.m. to 8.30 p.m.
United Churches Programme. Friary Park. Christian Brains Trust. 8.30 p.m.

Monday, July 12th.

Open Air Dancing. Friary Park. 7 p.m., Selma Dance Orchestra.
Brains Trust, Town Hall, 8 to 9 p.m. Question Master,
Lt.-Col. A. H. Farley, J.P.

Tuesday, July 13th.

Baby Show. Preliminary Judging. Friary Park. 3 to 5 p.m.
Mobile Cinema. War Savings Van. Friary Park. 6 to 9 p.m.
Open Air Dancing. Friary Park. 7 p.m. Selma Dance Orchestra.

Wednesday, July 14th.

Whist Drive. British Restaurant. Tickets, 1/6. 7 p.m.
Concert. Friary Park. 7.30 p.m.

Thursday, July 15th.

Civil Defence Exercise. Friary Park. 8 to 9 p.m.

Friday, July 16th.

Mobile Cinema. War Savings Van. Friary Park. 3 to 5 p.m.
Open Air Dancing. Friary Park. N.F.S. Orchestra. 7.30 p.m.

Saturday, July 17th.

'Appy 'Ampstead Fair. Friary Park. 2 p.m. OPENING DAY.
Dog Show. Friary Park. 3 p.m.
Plays by "Incognito." British Restaurant. 7.30 p.m.

Full particulars from F. T. TURNER, (Hon. Gen. Sec.), Town Hall, N.11.

An advertisement from the Finchley Press, *summer 1944.*

Local artistes gave freely of their time and talent as part of their contribution to the war effort. Some top-class shows resulted. Cyril Fletcher, whose father was Town Clerk of Friern Barnet, writes:

As I remember it, there were no fees for us – as the local product! The audiences were quite fabulous. Very appreciative and packed . . . My mother and father were living in Friern Barnet, my father being in charge of the ARP in that area in the cellar of the new town hall. He was aided by a Miss Askey – Arthur's sister. There was an odd happiness about those days if you tried not to think of how the ghastly macabre ambitions of those Nazi thugs were killing the youth and young genius of a whole generation.

CRIME AND PUNISHMENT

To the usual catalogue of crime familiar in our own day, the war years added numerous other classes of offences peculiar to those times. Perhaps the best known was the black market, which provided anything and everything in short supply – at a price. Such goods were mainly stolen. Places such as military stores and cookhouses were prime targets for the theft of foodstuffs in short supply which would finish up in local cafés and restaurants. Thefts of petrol were common, as were those of cigarettes and spirits such as whisky and gin. At Christmas time there might be the added spice of alcohol made in illicit stills!

It would seem that consciences could in most cases ignore what were regarded as harmless fiddles. The purchase of clothing coupons from those unable to afford new clothes (the going rate was 1s 6d per coupon) was a well-known example, as was the cultivation of the shopkeeper to provide an extra share of goods 'under the counter'.

The pages of the local newspaper contained numerous reports of offences:

Four deserters arrested in East Finchley cafe.

George C. charged with looting a carpet and a quantity of coal from a bombed building in Long Lane.

Fireman Thomas G. charged with stealing money from a bombed building.

Fred H., a butcher, charged with receiving 2 tins of corned beef, 16 pairs of grey socks, 11 brown blankets and 48 rounds of rifle ammunition knowing them to have been stolen.

Alfred V. was sent to prison for 2 months for stealing 2 cwt of potatoes, 44 chickens and 7 dozen eggs from the ABC Restaurant.

Mr S.N. fined 20 shillings for not immobilising his car.

J.A.R. of Whetstone fined 2 guineas on a summons that he, a registered person, failed to notify his change of address to the National Registration Officer.

Peter F. fined £50 plus 25 guineas costs, for selling chocolate covering at a price exceeding that of the controlled price.

Other offences included 'misuse of petrol' (£10 fine), 'failure to attend Home Guard parades', 'refusal to submit to a medical examination' (12 months' imprisonment) and 'using a different name' (£3 fine).

In a very different category were the conscientious objectors. They aroused strong feelings, as the *Finchley Press*'s editorial for 1 January 1943 indicates:

To dodgers, shirkers and conscientious objectors who refuse to help their country in any way, we most earnestly hope that, as early as possible in the New

Year, nemesis will overtake you. We regret that there are certain laws which prevent us from mentioning the real greeting we should like to give you.

Conscientious objectors were not cowards, though they were often subjected to ill-informed abuse. One remembers:

I am a Quaker, and wish to save life rather than to take it. When I reached 18, I was 'called-up' and registered as a Conscientious Objector. I joined the Friends Ambulance Unit. I received some training at Hammersmith Hospital, and was then posted to Germany with the invasion army. Many of my friends served as nurses at local military hospitals.

The multitude of laws and restrictions arising from the war, while irritating, were on the whole accepted in good part. It is difficult even today, however, to understand the bureaucratic warning issued to members of the WVS, church groups and the like about the illegality of raffling certain items. Such activities raised money for good causes such as the Red Cross, Aid to Russia Fund and the Merchant Navy Comfort Fund. Nevertheless, according to the caution 'there must be no raffling, auctioning or selling of baskets of fruit, vegetables, cakes or preserves. The Food Officer says this must cease because Retail Licences are required for sale of food and prices charged are frequently in excess of controlled prices.' The dictate was widely ignored.

Loose talk was also a punishable offence, as this extract from the *Hendon Times* of July 1941 shows:

A charge under the Defence Regulations of 'publishing a statement likely to cause alarm or despondency' was heard at Hendon Magistrates Court on Monday against L.W., a gas fitter employed at the Colindale works.

When an air raid siren sounded, he hurried with his colleagues to a nearby shelter. He said he thought that wars were a racket brought about by politicians for their own ends. He was hurried out of the shelter by some of the people there and arrested by P.S. Graves. For the defence, Mr R. Collett said that the defendant often went on like that, and they all took no notice of him. As stated L.W. was found guilty and fined £25.

SCHOOLS

The general panic caused early in the war by the threat of bombing also affected the schools. In common with all other public gatherings, schools were closed on 3 September 1939. The intention was to reduce casualties by dispersing the population. Some schools were used for specific civil defence purposes; most were earmarked as potential rest centres or refuges in case of an emergency, as schools have wide doorways to admit stretchers, a large hall for sorting an intake and good kitchen, toilet and washing facilities.

Our districts were not official evacuation areas, but many people nevertheless moved out of London. The attendances at Oakleigh Infants School, for example,

'Guaranteed to stop them talking'. These children are practising wearing their gas masks in a posed photograph taken for publicity purposes about October 1939. At this stage of the war paper crosses to stop flying glass had not been stuck onto classroom windows.

dropped from about 200 to 56 at one time. Schools were gradually reopened as shelter accommodation became available. These were generally made of concrete sewer pipes 8 ft in diameter, sunk into the ground and covered with soil.

Work was not always quick. In September 1938 Mr Verrinder noted that trenches were being dug in the playing field next to Underhill School. The trenches stayed, full of stagnant water, until the shelters were completed in April 1942.

The shelters at St James' School in Friern Barnet Lane were in the nearby playing field of Friern Barnet Grammar School, now part of Underhill Infants School. St John's School, Whetstone – at that time in Britannia Road, Finchley – used the shelters in Swan Lane Recreation Ground for a period. Stanhope Road

In the early days of the war trenches were dug for school children to shelter in. These were gradually replaced by purpose-built shelters.

School in Finchley had a brick-built surface shelter in the playground, which proved to be good for bouncing a ball against. Woodhouse School lost part of its 1st XI cricket pitch to the shelters, much to the despair of George Wood, the cricket master.

The shelters are recalled by one ex-pupil from All Saints' Girls School:

> The war started when I was at school, and I remember so well going to and from the air-raid shelters. My whole school life seems to have been spent singing 'Ten green bottles'. The shelters were in the spinney. They were like huge concrete sewer pipes covered in soil and grass. We went through a double door and sat on long slatted wooden bench seats facing each other – rather like on the underground. There were three or four shelters and each class had its own shelter. No one was frightened. I remember the siren sounding as I was on the way home to lunch and I jumped under a hedge. By the time I got home it was time to go back to school.

Sometimes the shelters weren't big enough and other arrangements had to be made, as this ex-pupil from Cromer Road School remembers:

> During the war sandbags were piled up along the corridor. We practised putting on our gas masks, which we carried at all times. I hated the smell of it. As there was not enough room for everyone in the shelter in the boiler room (or coke hole, as we called it), when the siren went we had to take it in turns either to sit among the sandbags in the corridor, or to sit among the coke downstairs. I could never understand why the Germans wanted to bomb our school. I remember my sadness on hearing that one of my classmates had been killed when a bomb fell on her house.

In common with many other schools with classrooms leading from a central corridor, Underhill and Cromer Road schools used large pieces of timber to shore up the ceilings in order to provide a refuge for some sixty children at a time. The children were supposed to lie down on the floor. The timber at Cromer Road was green and shrank so that the wood became loose. With typical ingenuity the teachers tied the timber up with string.

Some children were taught in small groups in their homes. Oakleigh Infants School, for example, had classes for about half a dozen children each at 36 St Margarets Avenue, 20 Russell Lane, 44 Queens Avenue and 37 Raleigh Drive. Another group of eighteen met in the parish hall, using the cellar of the vicarage as a shelter.

There was a good deal of confusion. When the head teacher of Cromer Road School was told that her central corridor was a refuge but not a shelter, she plaintively recorded 'No one will tell me the difference'. When the same head teacher asked for additional first-aid supplies, she was sent two packets of bandages and a packet of Elastoplast. She persuaded parents to send in old sheets that could be torn up into bandages if needed.

As the 'Phoney War' progressed more and more schools were able to reopen, often for a reduced period of part-time schooling. St John's, Whetstone and Underhill, Barnet opened in November 1939. Cromer Road had reopened on 24 October when the Head wrote 'May I point out an unexpected benefit of part-time schooling. With full-time staff and pupils only attending part-time, they get much more help than in ordinary classes of 44.' All windows were covered with crosses of sticky paper to reduce the danger from flying glass.

Woodhouse School reopened on 19 September 1939, with accommodation for sixty pupils. The junior pupils had two half-day sessions a week and the senior and sixth form pupils three sessions, made possible by working on Saturday mornings. The pupils were set homework for the other times.

All schools were working normally by January 1940.

At first the shelter accommodation was primitive, whether the shelter was brick-built or of concrete pipes. The children sat on benches placed against the side walls. The sanitation was usually a bucket hidden artistically behind a hessian screen at the end of the shelter. This inevitably caused interesting sound effects. In fact, lessons were subject to all sorts of disruption and difficulty, as this ex-pupil from Woodhouse School recalls:

> When the warning sounded, we picked up books, coats and gas mask cases and trotted along to our allotted shelter. Steps led down to a cold, damp and musty atmosphere. A bench ran along each side. Two classes shared each shelter and one would listen to their teacher's lesson while the other did written work. It was difficult to concentrate on algebra questions while a lesson on the Argentinian pampas was going on at the other end. Sometimes the lights would go out and then there was much giggling, scuffling and shrieking.

Many shelters leaked and were cold and damp. At Woodhouse School the craft and physics masters rigged up a system of electric lighting, though heating was always a problem. Pupils often had to lean against cold damp concrete walls. St James' School, among others, had the shelter lighting run from a separate meter which was read quarterly.

Many male teachers were called into the various services. John Davie, headmaster of Woodhouse wrote 'With only 4 masters and 14 mistresses, so much falls on the men, of whom Wood bears the brunt.' The men were replaced by teachers recalled out of retirement (and regrettably a few who should have stayed retired), but mainly from the reservoir of married women who returned to teaching, bringing with them a wealth of understanding about children.

During the Blitz of 1940/41 pupils lost much sleep and school hours were altered. The rule was that if there had been a raid during the night, school would not begin until 10.30 the following morning. This shortening of the school day was to have a cumulative effect so that by 1945 exam standards at age sixteen were about eighteen months behind those of 1939. Similarly, one junior school head teacher wrote that many eight-year-olds had not yet begun to read.

The school day was also, of course, disrupted by the raids themselves, as one St James' ex-pupil recalls:

One day we were sitting in the front classroom (you can still see it by the front door). We all heard a popping noise and looked up. Through the windows we actually saw bombs dropping. Incendiary bombs had been off-loaded and were falling all over the place. There was absolute panic as we all ran to the shelters behind the school. The sight of the caretaker putting a dustbin lid on a bomb in the playground is an indelible memory. While we were running, we heard a plane screaming low and then the siren sounded. Of course we enjoyed it as we did not realize the danger, and we did not have to do sums!

Fire-watching, that is having a person sleep in a building in order to deal with incendiary bombs, posed a particular problem for small schools. Monken Hadley School, for instance, had a staff of only four, yet it had to find someone every night to do fire-watch duty until it was incorporated into the street fire-watch system. In the secondary schools like Finchley County, Christ's College and Woodhouse the older boys helped. This was very popular as the pay was 1s 6d a night.

Because so many women were engaged in various kinds of war work, schools organized play centres during the holidays. These were run by teachers who regarded the work as their own particular contribution to the war effort.

All schools introduced school dinners which were encouraged by the government as part of the battle to improve nutrition. They became the source of many a tale. Some children love chocolate custard, others hate it. Some teachers forced every child to eat every mouthful. Others were more civilized. Meals were distributed by the teachers and eaten in the classrooms, which led to interesting problems like how to get mashed potato out of an ink well. Having to do compulsory dinner duty every day was a source of discontent amongst teachers for many years. School meals assistants were initially employed on a scale of one for 100 primary children and one for 300 older pupils.

The following extracts are from the log kept by Underhill Junior School; they would reflect wartime life at any school in the district:

1938 Sept: Gas masks fitted and checked for all our children.
1939 4 Sept: School opening delayed by the onset of war.
27 Nov: School reopened. Protective strips on windows.
1940 26 July: School closed for 2 weeks' holiday.
12 Aug: School reopened.
6 Sept: Air raids daily this week, morning & afternoon. Warning at 8.00. School opened at 10.30. 69 per cent attendance. 9-hour raid last night.
11 Sept: Raids – 11.55 to 12.15 and 3.10 to 4.30.
12 Sept: Heavy gun barrage last night.
25 Sept: Did not mark registers, only 107 present out of 367.
27 Sept:11.40 a.m. – Heard heavy gunfire & collected the children in the corridors.
9 Oct: Bomb damage to buildings to west of school. Our staff toilet ceiling has collapsed.
16 Oct: Time in classrooms this week 17½ hours.

1 Nov: Time in classrooms this week 16½ hours.

8 Nov: Time in classrooms this week 17 hours.

15 Nov: Time in classrooms this week 15 hours.

16 Nov: Two mines have devastated part of Barnet, Mrs Shears' house destroyed [a teacher, 6 West End Lane, Barnet], Mrs Shears not fit for work, 3 days' leave.

1941 6 Jan: Mr Smith [a teacher] called up, replaced by Mrs Hughes on supply.

Feb: No fires in school because shortage of coke, children sent home.

16 May: The rotting sandbag blast walls at the entrances have been rebuilt with new sandbags.

9 Nov: Fireguard duties organised, they will use the staff room. A party of children has made 8 visits to Wellhouse Hospital to entertain wounded soldiers.

1942 4 Feb: All children have been through the mobile gas chamber.

24 April: St George's day: saluting and cheering the Union Jack. We sang Land of Hope & Glory and the National Anthem.

1 June: 9 acres of our playing field have been ploughed up for food production.

Aug: Our play centre will have a small canteen serving snacks.

24 Oct: Half-term play centre & canteen open.

1943 4 March: The caretaker has flu. The cooks have been helping me to stoke the boilers.

8/9 June: The teachers are distributing cod liver oil & malt. Some children don't like it.

1944 8, 9, 10 Feb: The wardens checked the gas masks of all children.

16 June: Resumption of attacks on London by flying bombs.

19 June: Alert from dawn till 11.15 a.m.

22, 23 June: Most of day spent in shelters.

4 July: Only 30 minutes spent in the classrooms out of a whole day.

21 July: Only 37 children present.

1 Sept: Number on books 309, I have removed from the registers those I know have evacuated, leaving 214 present.

8 Nov: 62 scholars still evacuated.

1945 8 Jan: Caretaker ill. He had not ordered coke so no fires. 30 cwt arrived by fire engine and the firemen lit the boilers for me.

19 Jan: Still no coke, so school closed again.

8 May: End of the war in Europe, school flag hoisted, two days' holiday.

10 May: At a special assembly I addressed the children on 'The Dawn of a New Age'.

EVACUATION

The evacuation of children and other vulnerable people was a gigantic task, described by the then Ministry of Health as 'an exodus bigger than that of Moses'. Nationally, no less than 870,000 schoolchildren, 524,000 children under school age and 12,000 expectant mothers, along with 103,000 teachers and helpers were moved to 'safe areas'. County councils appointed billeting officers – some from the ranks of the local gentry and the WVS – to make arrangements. Much

Dennis – the evacuee whose story is told in the following pages.

has already been written about the successes and scandalous abuses that took place. The fact that the early months of the war were relatively quiet on the home front led many evacuees, bored and homesick, to return quickly to their own homes, very much against government advice.

Some evacuees were happy in their new homes. Others, such as this New Barnet child, were less fortunate:

I was born in 1935 and was about six years old when the air raids started. My father was in the Army and I was one of seven children looked after by my mother. I had no idea that I was to be evacuated – I did not know what it was or the meaning of the word. No one bothered to explain it to me. All I know is that we left home one morning to go to school. I carried my gas mask and had a label tied to my jacket. There were buses by the school and we were taken in them to New Barnet station where I got on a train with a younger brother and two of my sisters.

The train journey finished at Newcastle where we walked a short distance, hundreds of kids, to an assembly hall in a school. We were given a blanket, told to lie on the floor and go to sleep – it was dark by then and we had been travelling all day. In the morning, we went into another large hall where women came in and said 'I'll take that one' and went off with one of the children. It reminded me of a cattle market or choosing a chicken for dinner.

Every so often, someone would look us over and we would shout 'We're together.' No one wanted four children and at the end we were the only children left in the hall. Then three women came in: I think they may have been school cleaners. They said they would take us as they lived near to each other in a street called Grasmere Avenue, Walker Estate near Jesmond Park. We all got on a bus, and when we got off and were walking to our new homes a woman came out of a corner shop and asked 'Are these evacuees?', went back into the shop and came out with a cake for each of us.

We were then split up. My two sisters went with one of the women; my young brother went with another and he was just down the street from me. I went with Mrs Patterson. She took me into her house to show me round. 'This is the living room,' she said. 'Here is the front room which you keep out of at all times.' Upstairs she showed me the bedroom and told me that I would be sleeping between her two eighteen year old sons who did shift work in the shipyards of Newcastle. 'Now', she said 'you can go out and play.'

I knew no one. Up the road lived the boy whose parents had taken in my brother. He saw me and said that I would not see Tony any more, that he was now *his* brother. So I hit him hard and a fight started. His mother came out and parted us. She said I would not see my brother again, and I didn't until the time came to go back to London which was less than a year later.

Mrs Patterson was a hard woman who blamed me for anything that went wrong. The bed was terrible and I was squeezed between her sons like toothpaste from a tube, and it wasn't until much later that I had a bed of my own. I went to the local school about which I have few memories. It used a strap instead of the cane, and when the wind was in the right direction you could smell the toffee factory up at Wallsend. . . . Strange as it may seem, the local kids looked up to me because I came from London. When I had had that fight on the first day, another boy had been watching and asked if he could be a member of my gang. So I formed a gang and we were never bullied (neither did we bully other boys).

The food at home was very basic and I didn't really have enough to eat. I used to go to the local fish and chip shop and order a penn'orth of chips and 'crackling', which was a word they had never heard. All it was, as I explained, was the batter which had fallen from the fish and got crisped in the hot oil.

My two sisters lived in better conditions and used to visit me on occasions to keep me up with the news from home. My mother wrote to them but not to me. I didn't write home but relied upon my sisters. I remember that my mother sent some homemade sweets to my sisters with instructions to share them with me. I think they were made from powdered milk. I was eating one of the sweets when Mrs Patterson saw me and said 'What are you eating?' I explained it was a sweet from home and I think that it pricked her conscience. She asked 'Do you like sweets?' (what a question to ask a young child!) and said that she would make me some toffee – which she did. Unfortunately it burned in the pan and had a bitter taste but when she asked if I liked it I had to lie and say that it was nice. 'Good,' she said 'you can have the whole tin and it will be in the larder so you can help yourself at any time.'

As I learned later, my sisters had written home to say that none of us was happy in Newcastle. My mother saved enough money to pay for our fares back home and I suppose the journey back was the happiest experience of those years.

WAR WORK

The whole national effort was directed towards winning the war. Both men and women were conscripted to serve in the armed forces. Those who stayed behind were employed to help the war effort in factories large and small. The efforts varied from the boys of Woodhouse School making wooden boxes to hold engine parts, and a one-man business in Brunswick Park making washers, to large companies like the Standard Telephone Co. and Simms Motors. Other companies like Perry's Garage in North Finchley repaired or maintained service vehicles.

'The Standard' (STC)

The International Western Electric Telephone Company bought 27.5 acres of land in 1922 on a site near Oakleigh Road for £11,712. The company, which

Everything made at the Standard Factory, much of it secret, was important to the war effort – Bailey bridges, teleprinters, tank and fighter radios, transceivers for air-sea rescue launches and dinghies, blind-landing gear, and radio-operated predictors and automatic fuses for anti aircraft guns. Women made up a large part of the labour force.

The air raid precuations at the Standard Factory were said to be the finest in the country. In 1938 a series of fourteen tunnels, complete with escape hatches, was constructed by the 'cut and cover' method and provided shelter for the entire work force.

changed its name to Standard Telephones and Cables in 1925, soon became a world leader in the manufacture of land and underwater telecommunications equipment.

In 1938 the company built fourteen tunnels on the north end of the site for use as shelters in any emergency. These were built using the 'cut and cover' method, and were the subject of a feature by Richard Dimbleby on the Nine o'Clock News for 7 July 1939:

The shelter tunnels which have been dug under a part genuine, part built-up hill at one end of the works are among the most elaborate in the country. They have sanitary facilities and fresh drinking water and first-aid dugouts. They are proof even against direct hits and there are benches to accommodate every one of the works' employees. The 5,500 were down there for an hour today, calmly reading, talking, knitting or playing cards, and the temperature did not rise above 60 degrees because of the air conditioning. The tunnels, which are seven feet in diameter, have twelve entrances and three sloping emergency exits. They have three alternative systems of lighting, and telephones linking them to the world outside. They are, in fact, as safe as man can make them. So at last we have proof that a big plant can be cleared of its employees and can go into action at battleship speed. I think the moral of my report should be 'Other works, please copy'.

During the war, the company and its employees worked twenty-four hours a day in three shifts. Equipment made here included RADAR, ground-to-air signalling equipment, pulse beacons to aid bad weather landings, and radio sets. The company made most of the defence telecommunications network, which linked all home defences, including fighter and anti-aircraft commands, providing links with observer posts, guns, searchlights and airfields. Many thousands of miles of telephone wires were made up and installed.

Later special equipment was made to help jam the German radio beams which guided their aircraft, the 'Knickbein' system. Later still, radio sets were made to guide troops at the Normandy landings. For the D-Day landings a special telephone system was put into the headquarters comprising 30 positions, 260 exchange lines and 700 extensions.

At its peak, the Standard had about 14,000 employees, and spread its production facilities to other places in the district. One man, for example, manufactured washers in a lock-up garage. The rectifier section moved to a cabinet maker's in East Barnet and to Boreham Wood. Also used were a former eiderdown factory, part of a bottle factory (both close at hand), a printing works and part of a sweet factory.

The main factory had its own first-aid post, fire brigade, Home Guard unit and Territorial Army unit, called 'The Terriers'. As early as summer 1934 representations had been made for the formation of a special unit of the Royal Corps of Signals to be recruited from the employees of the New Southgate factory because of their close knowledge of the manufacture and use of communications equipment. By 1936 the unit consisted of three officers and about a hundred men, comprising two signals sections – J and L, both attached to the 44th Division. Some of the early recruits were issued with spurs, no doubt a relic of the cavalry days, and some fell downstairs as a result.

The unit practised hard, on two evenings a week, one whole Sunday a month and on annual summer camps. The company was very generous in giving the soldiers two weeks' leave, with pay, for the camp. In 1937 the unit was inspected by the then Princess Royal, and also formed part of the guard of honour when the proclamation of King Edward VIII was read at the town hall.

K.B. Baldwin of the staff joined the unit in 1937, and was with the section which went abroad and fought in the Middle East. He was promoted to Lieutenant-Colonel and awarded the MBE. He eventually became Honorary Colonel of the 44th (Home Counties) Divisional Signals Regiment (TA).

The factory's independent Home Guard unit protected the site, working closely with the existing civil defence staff. The unit worked on a six-day rota with six mobile platoons and six machine gun teams. Later equipment included two armoured cars, an armoured mobile Bofors anti-aircraft gun (with its own crews), and Bren and Lewis light machine guns. Like other local units, they also had Northover and Smith guns. The Bofors gun was fired only once in anger, and at extreme range, at a Heinkel 111.

The Standard Factory was draped in camouflage netting which went up in flames when the V1 hit. A number of workers who had taken refuge on a stairway were killed by the fire, for which the staircase acted a a chimney.

The unit was named 'B' Company of the 28th Battalion of the Middlesex Regiment. At that time it also covered part of the North Circular Road in accordance with the anti-invasion plans.

It was then decided that certain factories engaged on vital war work should have a much larger guard, and the STC unit was increased to about 400, with eight platoons on an eight-day rota and an HQ platoon. This company was transferred to the 29th Battalion of the Middlesex Regiment.

By November 1944, when the unit was 'stood down' the commanding officer was Major R. Moir, MC and the second-in-command was Captain D. Wain.

On the morning of 23 August 1944 a V1 flying bomb landed between buildings Six and Eight, demolishing the first and seriously damaging the second. It was the most serious incident in the district: 33 people were killed, about 212 seriously injured and about 218 slightly injured. On the evening of 24 August, a second V1 landed on the north sports field, but this time no one was hurt. C.E. Clarke, an STC employee, remembers the incident:

I was a 'mopper-up' with an orange and black armband. My job was to hurry the stragglers into the tunnels when the alarm sounded. This was soon abandoned because we lost so much production. A roof spotter was substituted, and at the last moment shouted 'Lay down' over the loud speaker system, and everyone threw themselves down under the benches.

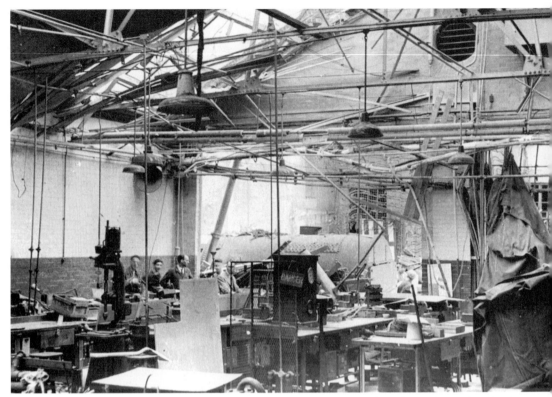

Eye witness account: 'About halfway along, where the bomb dropped in the roadway, the side of the building was smashed in. A rectangular supporting pillar 2 feet by 3 feet was stripped of concrete, leaving only the reinforcing rods and allowing the upper floor to sag.'

Two men, Bill Pace and Eddie Baker, who worked in George Richardson's 'Urgency' shop, were grand guys. Amongst many others who were hideously wounded on that day, each lost an eye. I remember, in the iron shop, stacks of steel sheets six feet by four scything through the air like a pack of playing cards, shredding everything in their path.

A First Aider present at the time recalled:

One young lady was lying on a stretcher with a brown smock draped over her legs. She said that her foot was hurting. I took off the smock to see what looked like a piece of raw meat with some almonds in it. She moved her leg, leaving the foot where it was, her leg started to pump blood. She was most distressed when I applied pressure to the femoral artery at the top of her thigh. I explained that I was married but was relieved when one of the female nurses took over. There was a middle aged chap from the carpenter's shop hobbling along with a large piece of wood through his thigh. He had sawed a piece off while it was still in his leg to enable him to get through the doorway.

FIVE

Preparations for Peace and the End of the War

PREPARATIONS FOR PEACE

During 1944, as an Allied victory began to look more and more certain, plans were being made to build a better Britain, just as had happened in 1918, and just as has happened with every government since the war ended. There were official working parties on subjects such as the future of the fire service, housing, drains and education. Many of these took place in response to government action like the 1944 Education Act and the Beveridge Report, which led to the creation of the Welfare State.

'Pre-fabs' in East Crescent, c. 1950.

One immediate problem was that of housing. In our district about 2,000 houses had been destroyed by enemy action, and a further 4,000 or so seriously damaged. There had of course been little new house building during the war, but with the end of hostilities in sight this deficiency could be addressed. Resources were limited but the aircraft industry had massive stocks of aluminium sheet and strip and considerable technical 'know how'. The result was the prefab – a house made from aluminium panels, pre-shaped in a factory and erected on site – based on a Canadian design. These were to prove very popular and, though intended to last only ten years, have proved capable of lasting into the 1990s.

THE END OF THE WAR

Early on the morning of 7 May 1945, at General Eisenhower's headquarters in Rheims, the German generals Jodl and von Friedeburg, acting for the German government, signed the surrender document. Fighting actually stopped at midnight on 8/9 May.

The war against Japan continued. Because it was so far away, it seemed to many at the time to be somehow less important in spite of the great suffering and heroism displayed. The Japanese surrender came into effect on 14 August after atomic bombs had been dropped on 6 August at Hiroshima and on 9 August at Nagasaki.

VE DAY

Victory in Europe was celebrated on 8 May, which was designated VE Day. Schools and most places of employment were given two days' holiday on 8 and 9 May.

There were, of course, massive and widespread celebrations. Typical were the celebrations in Finchley. Victory in Europe was celebrated at Avenue House in East End Road, Finchley by a crowd estimated at ten to fifteen thousand. The organizer was Mr S. Vernon-French. A special band called 'The Victory Serenaders', which played dancing music, included two members of Geraldo's orchestra.

One Whetstone resident recalled:

We walked from Whetstone along Friern Barnet Lane and Colney Hatch Lane to Alexandra Palace. It was our intention to look at the lights of London, which had been blacked out or dimmed for the past five years. Some houses had red, white and blue lamps in their front garden. Almost every house had its front-room lights blazing into the street. When we arrived at Ally Pally we formed part of a huge crowd, shouting, waving and singing 'There'll always be an England'.

Another Finchley resident said:

The next Saturday there was a street party. Tables were put out in the middle of the road and covered with tablecloths. There were sandwiches and cakes – I

The VE Day celebrations at Avenue House, East End Road, Finchley, attracted what was probably the biggest crowd to attend any local celebration. It is said that ten thousand people joined in the festivities.

Victory in Europe was widely celebrated by parades in May 1945. Here a detachment of sailors is marching along East Barnet Road near the junction with Henry Road.

The celebrations for VE Day included street parties. This one in Elm Park Road Finchley is typical. Trestle tables were set up down the middle of the road.

don't know where the mums got the rations from. Then all the kids sat down to eat. After that someone brought out a wind-up gramophone and there was dancing. I danced the waltz and trod on my partner's feet for the first time in my life that day.

The editorial comment for that day included this remark:

The war in the Far East, though, is very remote and does not affect us in the same way. Many thousands will hear with deep gratitude that members of their families are free from danger, but for some, the reaction has not got that sharp spur of personal interest.

VJ DAY

The end of the war against Japan was celebrated by VJ Day on 15 August. This was the cause of a further round of celebrations. The *Finchley Press* reported:

The VJ Day party in Squires Lane included a children's fancy dress competition. The judges were Mr & Mrs Dunn and Mr Williams. The winners were – Girls: M. Read, P. Williams, J. Goddard, H. Stretton. Boys: B. Goulding, B. Taylor, B. Scott, J. Watkins. Tiny Tots: J. Stoker, B. Nolan, P. Pound, S. Brown, S. Buxton. Music and fairy lights were provided by Mr J. Davies.

HOME AT LAST

On 15 October 1945 the *Finchley Press* was able to report good news about nurses from High Barnet and Finchley who had been missing on Java:

> Eleven Salvation Army nurses who had been working with lepers in the Dutch East Indies have been found. They had been out of contact for over three years and are now fit and well. They include Major Ellen Digby of East Finchley and majors Sarah Cullen and Sarah Robinson from High Barnet. The Japanese authorities had allowed them to continue working on condition that they treated Japanese soldiers as well.

Let the words of Revd M. Block, delivered at Finchley Synagogue in September 1945, form an endpiece to this book:

> For the past thirty-one years the tragedy has been that men have created false images in secret. The Spirit of God has been far from them. Thank God a new era has been ushered in, an era which calls for the very best from all human beings. We have fought not just for peace, but for the greatest happiness and well being for all.

Hendon's War Memorial in Watford Way, Hendon, pays tribute to the dead of two world wars and includes a special tablet to the memory of civilians killed during the Second World War.

Some Facts and Figures

THE SIZE AND COST OF CIVIL DEFENCE

By January 1940 East Barnet had recruited this amount of full-time staff:

Stretcher parties	120
Ambulances	15
Cars sitting wounded	12
4 × light rescue parties	44
4 × heavy rescue parties	28
Auxiliary firemen	95
Wardens	82
Total full-time staff	396

The total wages cost in a full financial year was £65,352 plus £21,063 for the fire service. This was by far the largest part of the council's budget, and compares with the next largest item of £15,000 for sewerage and £13,000 for the wages and salaries of all other staff.

In Finchley the figures were:

	Men	Women	Total
Wardens	631	158	789
First aid	240		240
First-aid posts	39	195	234
Drivers and crews for ambulances	216		216
Drivers for 24 cars	72		72
8 double crews light rescue	112		112
2 double crews heavy rescue	36		36
Anti-gas crews plus driver	56		56
Report/Control centre	18	42	60
Messengers	36		36
Auxiliary Fire Service	205		

In September 1939 the weekly wages bill for civil defence for Finchley was £2,314 and for the AFS £676.

Friern Barnet employed 575 women and 822 men on a full-time paid basis. That is a total of 1,397 out of a population (including children and pensioners) of about 18,000. There were many other part-time and voluntary helpers as well, nearly all of them women.

In September 1939 Hendon had 108 women and 36 men employed at the Control centres, with 90 messengers. There were 825 full-time and 975 part-time wardens. Forty-eight ambulance drivers were partnered by 48 attendants, and the 70-strong rescue teams worked alternate 24 hour shifts.

CASUALTIES AND DAMAGE

The available casualty figures are:

	Killed	Injured
Barnet	31	181
East Barnet	53	802
Finchley	76	336
Hendon	242	1,314

This was the scale of damage to housing (see also p. 16):

	Damage beyond repair	Serious damage	Slight damage
Barnet	157	375	4,987
East Barnet	200	405	13,878
Hendon	a total of 18,740 damaged or destroyed		

These are the figures for the number of bombs that fell in the area:

	Finchley	Hendon	Barnet	East Barnet
High explosive	213	579	144	98
Incendiary	126	261	1,600	3,700
Oil	14	39	12	11
Unexploded	39	70	–	–
Parachute mines	5	9	4	–
V1	7	8	5	7
V2	1	8	1	1

Total tonnage of bombs dropped on London and provincial towns during the Blitz:

London	7 Sep 1940 to 4 Nov 1940	13,600 tons
London	14 Nov 1940 to 16 May 1941	5,200 tons
Provincial towns	14 Nov 1940 to 16 May 1941	11,700 tons

This compares with 525,516 tons dropped by Bomber Command on Germany in 1944 alone, together with a further 387,501 tons dropped by the Americans.

Total 'alert' periods for the districts covered by this book:

1939	2 hrs	40 mins
1940	1,121 hrs	28 mins
1941	311 hrs	45 mins
1942	11 hrs	36 mins
1943	36 hrs	56 mins
1944	701 hrs	12 mins
1945	5 hrs	19 mins

This makes a grand total of 2,190 hours 56 minutes.

EVACUATION IN SUMMER 1944

Hendon had 5,518 applicants for evacuation during August and September 1944 – the height of the V1 raids. Of these, 4,699 actually travelled.

A census of shelter occupancy taken that year shows the effect of the evacuation:

Date	Public	School	Communal
31 July 1944	2,458	915	2,748
7 August 1944	2,430	971	2,546
14 August 1944	2,411	1,085	2,181
4 September 1944	1,026	468	974

Public shelters were those used casually and by anyone caught in the street during a raid. School shelters were intended to protect pupils and were not used in the evenings except in periods of great pressure. Communal shelters were designated to serve a particular factory, block of flats or district. They were often located in basements. They were organized by shelter marshals, and accommodation was often allocated to named persons.

Index

Page numbers given in italic refer to illustrations